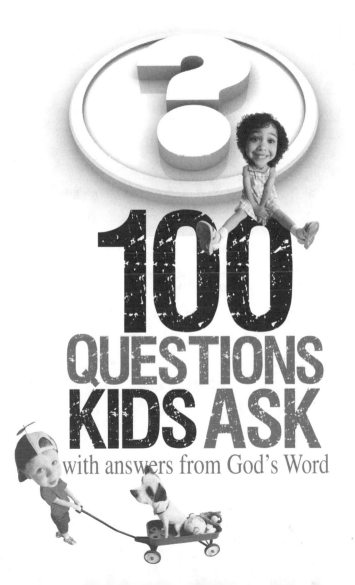

100 QUESTIONS KIDS ASK

with answers from God's Word

FAMILY
Christian Stores·

Scripture quotations are taken from:

The Holy Bible, King James Version (KJV)

The Holy Bible, New International Version (NIV) Copyright © 1973, 1978, 1984, by International Bible Society. Used by permission of Zondervan Publishing House. All rights reserved.

The Holy Bible, New King James Version (NKJV) Copyright © 1982 by Thomas Nelson, Inc. Used by permission.

Holy Bible, New Living Translation, (NLT) copyright © 1996. Used by permission of Tyndale House Publishers, Inc., Wheaton, Illinois 60189. All rights reserved.

The Message (MSG)- This edition issued by contractual arrangement with NavPress, a division of The Navigators, U.S.A. Originally published by NavPress in English as THE MESSAGE: The Bible in Contemporary Language copyright 2002-2003 by Eugene Peterson. All rights reserved.

New Century Version®. (NCV) Copyright © 1987, 1988, 1991 by Word Publishing, a division of Thomas Nelson, Inc. All rights reserved. Used by permission.

International Children's Bible®, New Century Version®. (ICB) Copyright © 1986, 1988, 1999 by Tommy Nelson™, a division of Thomas Nelson, Inc. All rights reserved. Used by permission.

The Holman Christian Standard Bible™ (HCSB) Copyright © 1999, 2000, 2001 by Holman Bible Publishers. Used by permission.

Cover Design Kim Russell / Wahoo Designs

Page Layout by Bart Dawson

ISBN 978-1-58334-007-3

Printed in the United States of America

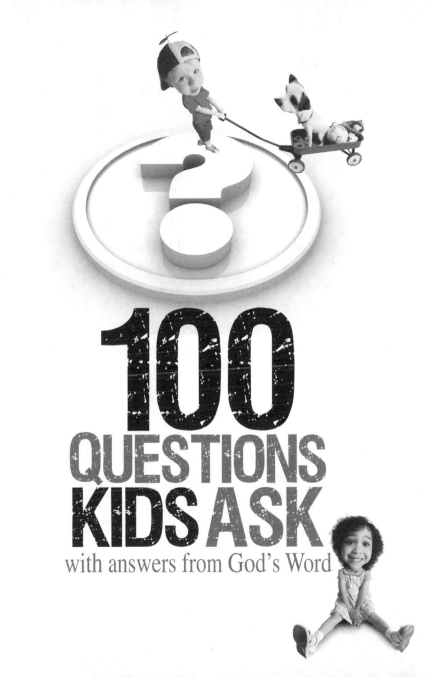

100 QUESTIONS KIDS ASK

with answers from God's Word

INDEX OF TOPICS

A Message to Parents

Perhaps your child's library is already overflowing with brightly colored children's books. If so, congratulations: you're a thoughtful parent who understands the importance of reading to young children.

This little book is an important addition to your child's library. It is intended to be read by Christian parents to their young children. The text contains 100 questions that kids ask, along with answers from God's Holy Word.

So try this experiment: read one or two chapters each night to your child, and then spend a few more moments talking about the things you've read. When you do, you'll make a lasting impression on your son or daughter, and that's a very good thing.

If you have been touched by God's love and His grace, then you know the joy that He has brought into your own life. Now it's your turn to share His message with the boy or girl whom He has entrusted to your care. Happy reading! And may God richly bless you and your family now and forever.

The Bible promises that God loves me. What should that mean to me?

THE QUICK ANSWER:

The fact that God loves you should make you a different kind of person—a better person, a more thankful person, and a happier person.

God Loves You

His banner over me was love.
Song of Solomon 2:4 KJV

If God had a refrigerator in heaven, your picture would be on it! And that fact should make you feel very good about the person you are and the person you can become.

God's love for you is bigger and more wonderful than you can imagine. So do this, and do it right now: accept God's love with open arms and welcome His

Son Jesus into your heart. When you do, you'll feel better about yourself . . . and your life will be changed forever.

A KID'S TIP

Remember: God's love for you is too big
to understand with your brain . . .
but it's not too big to feel
with your heart.

Jesus: the proof of God's love.

Philip Yancey

Everything I possess of any worth
is a direct product of God's love.

Beth Moore

Is the Bible really God's Word, or is it simply another book?

THE QUICK ANSWER:

The Bible is not just any old book—it is God's message to everybody in the world. The Bible contains the truth, and if you read it, that truth will speak to your heart.

The Bible . . . God's Message

Your word is like a lamp for my feet and a light for my way.
Psalm 119:105 ICB

What book contains God's Word? The Bible, of course. If you read the Bible every day, you'll soon be convinced that honesty is very important to God. And, since honesty is important to God, it should be important to you, too.

The Bible is the most important book you'll ever own. It's God's Holy Word. Read it every day, and follow its instructions. If you do, you'll be safe now and forever.

A KID'S TIP

Who's supposed to be taking care of your Bible? If it's you, then take very good care of it; it's by far the most important book you own!

The Bible is the treasure map that leads us to God's highest treasure: eternal life.

Max Lucado

The Bible became a living book and a guide for my life.

Vonette Bright

How powerful is God? Can He really perform miracles?

THE QUICK ANSWER:

God is so powerful that we cannot begin to understand His strength. He has the power to do anything—and that includes the power to perform big miracles, little miracles, or in between sized miracles.

God's Power

With God's power working in us, God can do much, much more than anything we can ask or imagine.
Ephesians 3:20 NCV

How strong is God? Stronger than anybody can imagine! But even if we can't understand God's power, we can respect His power. And we can be sure that God has the strength to guide us and protect us forever.

The next time you're worried or afraid, remember this: if God is powerful enough to create the universe and everything in it, He's also strong enough to take care of you. Now that's a comforting thought!

A KID'S TIP

Never be afraid to hope—
or to ask—for a miracle.

No giant will ever be a match for
a big God with a little rock.
Beth Moore

The task ahead of us is never as great
as the Power behind us.
Anonymous

What does the Bible say about the way I should treat the people in my family?

THE QUICK ANSWER:

The Bible makes it clear: you should give every member of your family love, respect, courtesy, and kindness.

My Family

Their first responsibility is to show godliness at home and repay their parents by taking care of them. This is something that pleases God very much.

1 Timothy 5:4 NLT

Sometimes, it's easiest to become angry with the people we love the most. After all, we know that they'll still love us no matter how angry we become. But while it's easy to become angry at home, it's usually wrong.

The next time you're tempted to become angry with a brother, or a sister, or a parent, remember that these are the people who love you more than anybody else! Then, calm down. Because peace is always beautiful, especially when it's peace at your house.

A KID'S TIP

Since you love your family, let them know it by the things you say and the things you do. And, never take your family members for granted; they deserve your very best treatment!

I like to think of my family as a big, beautiful patchwork quilt—each of us so different yet stitched together by love and life experiences.

Barbara Johnson

The first essential for a happy home is love.

Billy Graham

God has given me talents. What does He want me to do with those talents?

THE QUICK ANSWER:

God wants you to practice your talents and improve your skills . . . and He wants you to use your talents to make the world a better place.

God's Gift to You

God has given gifts to each of you from his great variety of spiritual gifts. Manage them well so that God's generosity can flow through you.
1 Peter 4:10 NLT

You're a very special person, a person with talents that have been given to you by God. So here's a question: will you use your talents or not? God wants you to use your talents to become a better person and a better Christian.

And that's what you should want for yourself.

And one more thing: while you're trying to figure out exactly what you're good at, be sure and talk about it with your parents. They can help you decide how best to use and improve the gifts God has given you.

A KID'S TIP

If you want to get better at something, practice a little. If you want to be outstanding, practice a lot.

Employ whatever God has entrusted you with, in doing good, all possible good, in every possible kind and degree.

John Wesley

What we are is God's gift to us. What we become is our gift to God.

Anonymous

If God is good, why does He allow bad things happen?

THE QUICK ANSWER:

Sometimes bad things happen because people do bad things. Sometimes bad things happen for reasons we don't understand. And it isn't God's job to explain why.

When Bad Things Happen

He heals the brokenhearted and bandages their wounds.
Psalm 147:3 NCV

If God is good, and if He made the world, why do bad things happen? Part of that question is easy to answer, and part of it isn't. Let's get to the easy part first: Sometimes, bad things happen because people choose to disobey God's rules.

When people break the rules—especially God's rules—they invite sadness and trouble into our beautiful world; it's unfortunate but it happens.

But on other occasions, bad things happen, and it's nobody's fault. So who is to blame then? Sometimes, nobody is to blame. Sometimes, things just happen and we simply cannot know why. Thankfully, all our questions will be answered . . . some day.

The good news is this: the Bible promises that when we finally get to heaven, we will understand all the reasons behind God's plans. But until then, we must simply trust Him.

A KID'S TIP

Remember: through good times and bad,
God is always with you,
and you are always protected.

Sometimes, I don't feel like sharing the things I have. What does the Bible say about that?

THE QUICK ANSWER:

It's simple: God wants you to be a generous person—and that means sharing your things even if you'd rather not.

Sharing Our Stuff

God loves a cheerful giver.
2 Corinthians 9:7 NIV

Jesus told us that we should be generous with other people, but sometimes we don't feel much like sharing. Instead of sharing the things that we have, we want to keep them all to ourselves. But God doesn't want selfishness to rule our hearts; He wants us to be generous.

Are you lucky enough to have nice things? If so, God's instructions are clear: you must share your blessings with others. And that's exactly the way it should be. After all, think how generous God has been with you.

A KID'S TIP

When am I old enough to start giving?
If you're old enough to understand these words, you're old enough to start giving to your church and to those who are less fortunate than you.
If you're not sure about the best way to do it, ask your parents!

What is your focus today?
Joy comes when it is Jesus first, others second . . . then you.

Kay Arthur

Don't be afraid to share
what you have with others;
after all, it all belongs to God anyway.

Jim Gallery

Sometimes, I get angry. What does the Bible say about anger?

THE QUICK ANSWER:

The Bible warns that anger can lead to danger (in fact, anger is only one letter away from danger!). Anger can also make you very unhappy . . . so it's important to learn ways to control your temper.

An Anger Alert

My dear brothers, always be willing to listen and slow to speak. Do not become angry easily. Anger will not help you live a good life as God wants.

James 1:19 ICB

Temper tantrums are so silly. And so is pouting. So, of course, is whining. When we lose our tempers, we say things that we shouldn't say, and we do things that we shouldn't do. Too bad!

The Bible tells us that it is foolish to become angry and that it is wise to remain calm. That's why we should learn to control our tempers before our tempers control us.

A KID'S TIP

Count to ten . . . but don't stop there! If you're angry with someone, don't say the first thing that comes to your mind. Instead, catch your breath and start counting until you are once again in control of your temper. If you count to a thousand and you're still counting, go to bed! You'll feel better in the morning.

Anger is the noise of the soul; the unseen irritant of the heart; the relentless invader of silence.

Max Lucado

When I do things that disappoint God, does He forgive me?

THE QUICK ANSWER:

It's simple: when you ask God to forgive you, He does it. God will forgive you every time you ask.

Asking for Forgiveness

If we say we have no sin, we are fooling ourselves, and the truth is not in us. But if we confess our sins, he will forgive our sins, because we can trust God to do what is right. He will cleanse us from all the wrongs we have done.

1 John 1:8-9 NCV

How often does God forgive us? More times than we can count! And that, by the way, is exactly how many times that God expects us to forgive other people—more times than we care to count.

Of this you can be sure: God won't ever get tired of forgiving you. And, because He has forgiven you, He doesn't want you to get tired of forgiving other people . . . ever!

A KID'S TIP

Because God has forgiven you, you can forgive others.

Every time we forgive others, deserving it or not, we have a reminder of God's forgiveness.

Franklin Graham

God does what few men can do— forgets the sins of others.

Anonymous

How does God want me and my friends to behave?

THE QUICK ANSWER:

God wants you to obey His rules and your parents' rules. And when you do, you'll be rewarded for your good behavior.

Good Behavior

Even a child is known by his behavior. His actions show if he is innocent and good.

Proverbs 20:11 ICB

Doing the right thing is not always easy, especially when we're tired or frustrated. But, doing the wrong thing almost always leads to trouble. And sometimes, it leads to BIG trouble.

When you do the right thing, you don't have to worry about what you did or what you said. But, if you are dishonest—or if you do something that you know is wrong—you'll be worried that someone will find out. So do the right thing; it may be harder in the beginning, but it's easier in the end.

A KID'S TIP

Good behavior leads to a happy life.
And bad behavior doesn't.
Behave accordingly.

God has "wired" us in such a way that
the more righteous we are,
the more we'll actually enjoy life.

Bill Hybels

There may be no trumpet sound or loud applause when we make a right decision, just a calm sense of resolution and peace.

Gloria Gaither

Sometimes, I feel like I don't measure up. What should I do?

THE QUICK ANSWER:

Sometimes you may feel like you're not "good enough." But God and your parents love you just the way you are—and you should love yourself, too. You don't have to be perfect to be wonderful!

You're Wonderfully Made

For you created my inmost being . . .
I praise you because I am fearfully
and wonderfully made . . . .
Psalm 139:13-14 NIV

The Bible teaches you this lesson: you should love everybody—and the word "everybody" includes yourself. Do you treat yourself with honor and respect? You should. After all, God created you in a very special way, and He loves you very much. And if God thinks you are amazing and wonderful, shouldn't you think about yourself in the same way? Of course you should!

God wants you to love everybody, including the person you see when you look in the mirror. And one more thing: when you learn how to respect the person in the mirror, you'll be better at respecting other people, too.

A KID'S TIP

If you hear a little voice inside your head telling you that you're not good enough . . . don't pay attention to that little voice. God loves you . . . and if you're good enough for God, you're good enough.

Being loved by Him whose opinion matters most gives us the security to risk loving, too—even loving ourselves.

Gloria Gaither

When I'm disappointed with the way things have turned out, what should I do?

THE QUICK ANSWER:

If you're unhappy about something, you can talk to your parents and you can talk to God . . . and that's exactly what you should do!

Overcoming Disappointment

Do not be afraid or discouraged, for the LORD is the one who goes before you. He will be with you; he will neither fail you nor forsake you.

Deuteronomy 31:8 NLT

Some days are more wonderful than other days. Sometimes, everything seems to go right, and on other days, many things seem to go wrong. But here's something to remember: even when you're disappointed with the way things turn out, God is near . . . and He loves you very much!

If you're disappointed, worried, sad, or afraid, you can talk to your parents and to God. And you will certainly feel better when you do!

A KID'S TIP

Things Didn't Work Out?
When you're disappointed about something, you can always talk to your parents . . . and you should!

The next time you're disappointed, don't panic. Don't give up.
Just be patient and let God remind you he's still in control.

Max Lucado

A brook would lose its song if God removed the rocks.

Anonymous

What does the Bible say about the kind of relationship that I should have with Jesus Christ?

THE QUICK ANSWER:

God wants you to have a close relationship with Jesus. That means that you should be a person who really tries to do what Jesus says.

Your Relationship with Jesus

Whoever serves me must follow me. Then my servant will be with me everywhere I am. My Father will honor anyone who serves me.

John 12:26 NCV

Whether you realize it or not, you already have a relationship with Jesus. Hopefully, it's a close relationship! Why? Because the friendship you form with

Jesus will help you every day of your life . . . and beyond!

You can either choose to invite Him into your heart, or you can ignore Him altogether. Welcome Him today—and while you're at it, encourage your friends and family members to do the same.

A KID'S TIP

If you want to follow in Christ's footsteps . . . welcome Him into your heart, obey His commandments, and share His never-ending love.

We have in Jesus Christ a perfect example of how to put God's truth into practice.

Bill Bright

In the dark? Follow the Son.

Anonymous

Sometimes it's hard for me to forgive the people who have hurt me. What does the Bible say about forgiveness?

THE QUICK ANSWER:

The Bible says that you've got to forgive other people . . . even when it's hard.

Forgiveness

I tell you, love your enemies. Pray for those who hurt you. If you do this, you will be true sons of your Father in heaven.

Matthew 6:44-45 ICB

How hard is it to forgive people? Sometimes, it's very hard! But God tells us that we must forgive other people, even when we'd rather not forgive them. So, if you're angry with anybody (or if you're upset by something you yourself have done), it's time to forgive.

God instructs us to treat other people exactly as we wish to be treated. When we forgive others, we are obeying our Heavenly Father, and that's exactly what we must try to do.

A KID'S TIP

If you're having trouble forgiving someone else . . . think how many times other people have forgiven you!

Only the truly forgiven
are truly forgiving.
C. S. Lewis

Learning how to forgive and forget
is one of the secrets of
a happy Christian life.
Warren Wiersbe

What is heaven going to be like?

THE QUICK ANSWER:

We don't know exactly what heaven will be like, but we do know that it will be wonderful. And how do we know that? Because God says so in the Bible!

Heaven Is Wonderful

Since you have been raised to new life with Christ, set your sights on the realities of heaven, where Christ sits at God's right hand in the place of honor and power.

Colossians 3:1 NLT

The Bible makes this important promise: when you give your heart to Jesus, you will live forever with Him in heaven. And Jesus told us that His house has "many mansions" (John 14:1-3).

Even though we don't know everything about heaven, we do know this: heaven will be a wonderful place, a place of joy and wonder, a place where we will be reunited with our loved ones and with God. It's wonderful to think about . . . and it's a priceless gift from God.

A KID'S TIP

Heaven is all those wonderful things
you wish you had on earth . . .
and much, much, much, much more.

As Catherine of Siena said,
"All the way to heaven is heaven."
A joyful end requires a joyful means.
Bless the Lord.
Eugene Peterson

Knowing where you are going takes
the uncertainty out of getting there.
Anne Graham Lotz

Sometimes I don't feel like being cheerful. What does the Bible say about being cheerful?

THE QUICK ANSWER:

The Bible encourages you to be a cheerful Christian. And when you stop to think about it, don't you have lots of things to be cheerful about? Of course you do!

Choose to Be Cheerful

A joyful heart makes a face cheerful.
Proverbs 15:13 HCSB

The Bible tells us that a cheerful heart is like medicine: it makes us feel better. Where does cheerfulness begin? It begins inside each of us; it begins in the heart. So let's be thankful to God for His blessings, and let's show our thanks by sharing good cheer wherever we go.

Today, make sure that you share
a smile and a kind word with as many
people as you can. This old world needs
all the cheering up it can get . . . and so
do your friends.

A KID'S TIP

Do you need a little cheering up?
Cheer up somebody else.
When you brighten somebody else's day,
you brighten up your own day, too.

We may run, walk, stumble, drive, or fly,
but let us never lose sight of the reason
for the journey, or miss a chance
to see a rainbow on the way.

Gloria Gaither

When we bring sunshine into the lives
of others, we're warmed by it ourselves.
When we spill a little happiness,
it splashes on us.

Barbara Johnson

What does the Bible say about doing the right thing?

THE QUICK ANSWER:

The Bible says this: God wants you to do the right thing; your parents want you to do the right thing; and you should want to do the right thing, too. So do everybody a favor—when you know what you're supposed to do, do it!

The Right Thing

But now you are children of God who obey. Be holy in all that you do, just as God is holy.

1 Peter 1:14-15 ICB

In the Book of Proverbs, King Solomon gave us wonderful advice for living wisely. Solomon said that we should keep our eyes "focused on what is right." In other words, we should do our best to say and do the things that we know are pleasing to God.

The next time you're tempted to say an unkind word or to say something that isn't true, remember the advice of King Solomon. Solomon knew that it's always better to do the right thing, even when it's tempting to do otherwise. So if you know something is wrong, don't do it; instead, do what you know to be right. When you do, you'll be saving yourself a lot of trouble and you'll be obeying the Word of God.

A KID'S TIP

If you're not sure it's the right thing to do . . . listen to your conscience and talk to your parents.

When we do what is right, we have contentment, peace, and happiness.

Beverly LaHaye

I've heard lots of things about angels, but are they real?

THE QUICK ANSWER:
The Bible says that angels are real . . . very real.

God's Angels

For He will give His angels orders concerning you, to protect you in all your ways.
Psalm 91:11 HCSB

The Bible has a lot to say about angels. But maybe you've wondered if angels are really real. If so, wonder no more! If the Bible tells you something, you can be sure that it's true.

The Bible teaches us that angels come from God, so that means they are good and they are helpful. So we don't need to fear angels . . . but neither do we need to pretend that they don't exist!

A KID'S TIP

If you believe what's in the Bible . . .
then you believe in angels!

I believe in angels because
the Bible says there are angels;
and I believe the Bible to be
the true Word of God.

Billy Graham

Angels descending,
bring from above,
echoes of mercy,
whispers of love.

Fanny Crosby

Sometimes, it's hard for me to be patient. What does the Bible say about that?

THE QUICK ANSWER:
The Bible teaches that patience is good and impatience isn't.

Please Be Patient

Patience is better than strength.
Proverbs 16:32 ICB

The Book of Proverbs tells us that patience is a very good thing. But for most of us, patience can also be a very hard thing. After all, we have many things that we want, and we want them NOW! But the Bible tells us that we must learn to wait patiently for the things that God has in store for us.

Are you having trouble being patient? If so, remember that patience takes practice, and lots of it, so keep trying. And if you make a mistake, don't be too upset. After all, if you're going to be a really patient person, you shouldn't just be patient with others, you should also be patient with yourself.

A KID'S TIP

An important part of growing up is learning to be patient with others and with yourself. And one more thing: learn from everybody's mistakes, especially your own.

If only we could be as patient with other people as God is with us!

Jim Gallery

God gave everyone patience— wise people use it.

Anonymous

Sometimes I don't really feel like going to church. What does the Bible say about church?

THE QUICK ANSWER:

God wants you to attend church. And so do your parents. So whenever you get the chance to go to church, please don't complain about going!

Attending Church

For where two or three come together in my name, there am I with them.

Matthew 18:20 NIV

When your parents take you to church, are you pleased to go? Hopefully so. After all, church is a wonderful place to learn about God's rules.

The church belongs to God just as surely as you belong to God. That's why the church is a good place to learn about God and about His Son Jesus.

So when your mom and dad take you to church, remember this: church is a fine place to be . . . and you're lucky to be there.

A KID'S TIP

Ignore the excuses. If somebody starts making up reasons not to go to church, don't pay any attention . . . even if that person is you!

Only participation in the full life of a local church builds spiritual muscle.

Rick Warren

In God's economy you will be hard-pressed to find many examples of successful "Lone Rangers."

Luci Swindoll

Sometimes, I am afraid. What does the Bible say about fear?

THE QUICK ANSWER:

You can always take your fears to your parents and to God.

When You're Afraid

I asked the Lord for help,
and he answered me.
He saved me from all that I feared.

Psalm 34:4 ICB

When bad things happen, it's understandable that we might feel afraid. In fact, it's good to be afraid if our fears keep us from behaving foolishly (by the way, if that little voice inside your head tells you that doing something is dangerous, don't do it).

When our own troubles—or the world's troubles—leave us fearful, we should discuss our concerns with the people who love and care for us. Parents and grandparents can help us understand our fears, and they can help us feel better. That's why we need to talk with them. We should also discuss our worries with our Heavenly Father. God is always ready to hear our prayers, and He can give us comfort when we feel afraid.

It's okay to be afraid—all of us are fearful from time to time. And it's good to know that we can talk about our fears with loved ones and with God. When we do, we'll discover that fear lasts for a little while, but love lasts forever.

A KID'S TIP

Don't keep your feelings bottled up inside . . . when something is bothering you, talk things over with your parents.

When I'm worried about things, what should I do?

THE QUICK ANSWER:

If you're worried about something, talk to your parents and talk to God. And keep talking until you feel better!

Don't Worry

Do not worry about anything. But pray and ask God for everything you need.
Philippians 4:6 ICB

When we're worried, there are two places we should take our concerns: to the people who love and care for us and to God.

When troubles arise, it helps to talk about them with parents, grandparents, and concerned adults. But we shouldn't stop there: we should also talk to God through our prayers.

If you're worried about something, you can pray about it anytime you want. And remember that God is always listening, and He always wants to hear from you.

So when you're worried, try this plan: talk and pray. Talk to the grownups who love you, and pray to the Heavenly Father who made you. The more you talk and the more you pray, the better you'll feel.

A KID'S TIP

Don't keep your feelings bottled up inside. If something makes you uncomfortable, scared, or worried, tell your parents . . . right now!

Worry is a complete waste of energy. It solves nothing. And it won't solve that anxiety on your mind either.
Charles Swindoll

I have lots of things to be thankful for. What should I do?

THE QUICK ANSWER:

Say "Thank you" . . . to your family (especially your parents), to your friends, and to God!

Saying Thanks

I will give You thanks with all my heart.
Psalm 138:1 HCSB

If you sat down and began counting your blessings, how long would it take? A very, very long time! Your blessings include your life, your family, your friends, your talents, and possessions, for starters. But, your greatest blessing—a gift that is yours for the asking—is God's gift of eternal life through Christ Jesus.

You can never count up every single blessing that God has given you, but it doesn't hurt to try . . . so get ready, get set, go—start counting your blessings RIGHT NOW!

A KID'S TIP

Those two special words: Thank you! Your parents and your teachers will never become tired of hearing those two little words. Say them often.

It is always possible to be thankful for what is given rather than to complain about what is not given. One or the other becomes a habit of life.

Elisabeth Elliot

A spirit of thankfulness makes all the difference.

Billy Graham

What should Christ's love mean to me?

THE QUICK ANSWER:

The fact that Jesus loves you means that you should love Him, too. And you should try your best to do the things He wants you to do.

Jesus Loves Me

Just as the Father has loved Me, I also have loved you. Remain in My love.
John 15:9 HCSB

Perhaps you've heard these words before: "Jesus loves me, this I know, for the Bible tells me so." Of course, these words can be found in the song "Jesus Loves Me." It's a wonderful song that should remind you of something very important: Jesus loves you very much.

When you invite Jesus to become your friend, He will do it . . . and He'll be your friend forever. If you make mistakes, He'll still be your friend. If you misbehave, He'll still love you. If you feel sorry or sad, He can help you feel better.

Yes, Jesus loves you more than you know. And when you welcome Him into your heart, you will be blessed now and forever.

A KID'S TIP

Jesus loves you . . . His love is amazing, it's wonderful, and it's meant for you.

The richest meaning of your life is contained in the idea that Christ loved you enough to give His life for you.

Calvin Miller

I'm a very lucky person. What should I do about it?

THE QUICK ANSWER:

You should thank God every day for His blessings.

Be Quick to Thank God

Thank God for this gift, his gift. No language can praise it enough!
2 Corinthians 9:15 MSG

Are you a thankful person? You should be! Whether you realize it or not, you have much to be thankful for. And who has given you all the blessings you enjoy? Your parents are responsible, of course. But all of your blessings really start with God.

All of us should make thanksgiving a habit. Since we have been given so much, the least we can do is say "Thank

You" to the One who has given us more blessings than we can possibly ever count.

A KID'S TIP

When is the best time to say "thanks" to God? Anytime. God loves you all the time, and that's exactly why you should praise Him all the time.

This is my story, this is my song, praising my Savior, all the day long.
Fanny Crosby

The Bible instructs—and experience teaches—that praising God results in our burdens being lifted and our joys being multiplied.
Jim Gallery

I know I should be kind to other people. But what if it's hard to be kind?

THE QUICK ANSWER:
Even when it's hard to be kind, you must try to be kind! No exceptions.

Kindness Is Cool

Kind words are like honey—sweet to the soul and healthy for the body.
Proverbs 16:24 NLT

An attitude of kindness starts in your heart and works its way out from there.

Do you listen to your heart when it tells you to be kind to other people? Hopefully, you do. After all, lots of people in the world aren't as fortunate as you are—and some of these folks are living very near you.

Ask your parents to help you find ways to do nice things for other people.

And don't forget that everybody needs love, kindness, and respect, so you should always be ready to share those things, too.

A KID'S TIP

You can't just talk about it. In order to be a kind person, you must do kind things—your kind thoughts must be translated into kind actions.

As you're rushing through life, take time to stop a moment, look into people's eyes, say something kind, and try to make them laugh!

Barbara Johnson

When you extend hospitality to others, you're not trying to impress people, you're trying to reflect God to them.

Max Lucado

When I feel sad, what should I do?

THE QUICK ANSWER:
That's simple: talk to your parents about your feelings!

Feeling Sad?

Those people who know they have great spiritual needs are happy, because the kingdom of heaven belongs to them. Those who are sad now are happy, because God will comfort them.

Matthew 5:3-4 NCV

Sometimes, you feel happy, and sometimes you don't. When you're feeling sad, here are two very important things you should do: 1. Talk to your parents about your feelings. 2. Talk to God about your feelings.

Talking with your parents is helpful because your mom and dad understand this: The problems that seem VERY BIG to you today probably won't seem so big tomorrow.

Talking with God helps because God hears your prayers and He helps make things better.

So the next time you're sad, don't hold your feelings inside—talk things over with your parents and with God. When you do, you'll feel better . . . and so will they!

A KID'S TIP

Sometimes happy, sometimes sad: Even if you're a very good person, you won't be happy all the time. Sometimes, things will happen to make you sad, and it's okay to be sad when bad things happen to you, to your friends, or to your family. But remember: through good times and bad, God is always with you, and you are always protected.

What does the Bible say about obeying my parents?

THE QUICK ANSWER:

Your parents know what's best for you. That's why God wants you to obey your parents.

Obeying God and Parents

Children, obey your parents in the Lord, for this is right.

Ephesians 6:1 NIV

When your parents ask you to do something, do you usually obey them or do you usually ignore them? When your parents try to get your attention, do you listen or not? When your parents make rules, do you obey those rules or do you break them? Hopefully, you've learned to listen to your parents and to obey.

When you learn the importance of obedience, you'll soon discover that good things happen when you behave yourself. And the sooner you learn to listen and to obey, the sooner those good things will start happening . . . to you!

A KID'S TIP

Since you love your family . . .
show it by behaving yourself
and obeying your family's rules!

The child that never learns to obey
his parents in the home will not obey
God or man out of the home.
Susanna Wesley

God uses ordinary people
who are obedient to Him to do
extraordinary things.
John Maxwell

Sometimes I say things that I shouldn't say. What does the Bible teach me about the way that I should talk to other people?

THE QUICK ANSWER:

God wants you to say nice things, and He wants you to try to think about the things you say before you say them!

Think Before You Speak

Let the words of my mouth,
and the meditation of my heart,
be acceptable in thy sight, O Lord,
my strength and my redeemer.
Psalm 19:14 KJV

Sometimes, it's easier to say the wrong thing than it is to say the right thing—especially if we're in a hurry to blurt out the first words that come into our heads. But, if we are patient and if we choose our words carefully, we can help other people feel better, and that's exactly what God wants us to do.

The Book of Proverbs tells us that the right words, spoken at the right time, can be wonderful gifts to our families and to our friends. That's why we should think about the things that we say before we say them, not after. When we do, our words make the world a better place, and that's exactly what God wants!

A KID'S TIP

Stop, think, then speak: If you want to make your words useful instead of hurtful, don't open your mouth until you've turned on your brain.

Change the heart,
and you change the speech.
Warren Wiersbe

What does the Bible say about God's love?

The Bible says many things about God, but here's one thing you should never forget: God is love, and He loves you!

God's Love

We know how much God loves us,
and we have put our trust in him.
God is love, and all who live in love
live in God, and God lives in them.

1 John 4:16 NLT

Does God love you? Of course He does! In fact, God loves you so much that He sent His Son Jesus to come to this earth . . . for you! When you accept Jesus into your heart, God gives you a gift that is more precious than gold: that gift is called "eternal life" which means that you will live forever with God in heaven!

You don't have to be perfect to earn God's love . . . you simply have to accept His love by accepting His Son. So do yourself a favor right now: accept God's love with open arms and welcome His Son Jesus into your heart. When you do, your life will be changed today, tomorrow, and forever.

A KID'S TIP

Remember: God's love for you is too big
to understand with your brain . . .
but it's not too big to feel
with your heart.

He created us because He delights in us!
Beth Moore

God proved his love on the cross.
Billy Graham

Jesus loves me. What should I do about Christ's love?

THE QUICK ANSWER:

You should welcome Jesus into your heart, and you should do your best to obey His rules today and every day.

Following Jesus

Whoever serves me must follow me. Then my servant will be with me everywhere I am. My Father will honor anyone who serves me.

John 12:26 NCV

The Bible makes this promise: Jesus loves you. And how should that make you feel? Well, the fact that Jesus loves you should make you very happy indeed, so happy, in fact, that you try your best to do the things that Jesus wants you to do.

Jesus wants you to welcome Him into your heart, He wants you to love and obey God, and He wants you to follow His example. He's done His part . . . and the rest is up to you!

A KID'S TIP

If you want to follow in Christ's footsteps . . . welcome Him into your heart, obey His commandments, and share His never-ending love.

I can tell you, from personal experience of walking with God for over fifty years, that He is the Lover of my soul.

Vonette Bright

Peter said, "No, Lord!" But he had to learn that one cannot say "No" while saying "Lord" and that one cannot say "Lord" while saying "No."

Corrie ten Boom

How important is money and the stuff money can buy?

THE QUICK ANSWER:

The Bible says that our lives are not measured by how much stuff we have. Our lives are measured by how much we love other people, and how much we honor God.

Stuff Isn't That Important!

Then Jesus said to them, "Be careful and guard against all kinds of greed. A man's life is not measured by the many things he owns."

Luke 12:15 ICB

Here's something to remember about stuff: It's not that important!

Lots of people are in love with money and the things that money can buy. God is not. God cares about people, not possessions, and so must you.

You should not be too concerned about the clothes you wear, or the things you own. And above all, don't ever let your self-esteem depend upon the things that you (or your parents) own.

The stuff that you own isn't nearly as important as the love that you feel in your heart—love for your family, love for your friends, and love for your Father in heaven.

A KID'S TIP

If you find yourself focusing too much on stuff, try spending a little less time at the mall and a little more time talking to God.

We own too many things that aren't worth owning.

Marie T. Freeman

If you really want to know God, how should you behave?

THE QUICK ANSWER:
You should love other people.

God Is Love

Whoever does not love does not know God, because God is love.
1 John 4:8 ICB

In the Bible, God makes this amazing promise—He promises that He loves you.

And it's a promise that He intends to keep.

No matter where you are (and no matter what you've done), you're never beyond the reach of God's love. So take time today (and every day) to thank Him for love that is too big to understand with your head, but not too big to feel with your heart.

A KID'S TIP

When you learn about the Bible,
you'll learn how much God loves you.

I am convinced our hearts are not
healthy until they have been satisfied
by the only completely healthy love that
exists: the love of God Himself.
Beth Moore

God's promises are overflowings
from his great heart.
C. H. Spurgeon

I am part of God's family. How should I treat others?

THE QUICK ANSWER:

Show respect to your family, to your friends, and to the people you meet every day.

Respect Other People

Show respect for all people. Love the brothers and sisters of God's family.

1 Peter 2:17 ICB

Are you polite and respectful to your parents and teachers? And do you do your best to treat everybody with the respect they deserve? If you want to obey God's rules, then you should be able to answer yes to these questions.

Remember this: the Bible teaches you to be a respectful person—and if it's right there in the Bible, it's certainly the right thing to do!

A KID'S TIP

Speak respectfully to everybody,
starting with parents, grandparents,
teachers, and adults . . . but don't stop
there. Be respectful of everybody,
including yourself!

If you are willing to honor a person out
of respect for God, you can be assured
that God will honor you.

Beth Moore

If we have the true love of God in our
hearts, we will show it in our lives.
We will not have to go up and down
the earth proclaiming it. We will show
it in everything we say or do.

D. L. Moody

I'm just a kid. How can I really be a good example to other people?

THE QUICK ANSWER:

No matter how old you are, you can still be a good example to your friends and family. So as you decide how you're going to behave, remember that young people are examples, too.

What Kind of Example Are You?

You are young, but do not let anyone treat you as if you were not important. Be an example to show the believers how they should live. Show them with your words, with the way you live, with your love, with your faith, and with your pure life.

1 Timothy 4:12 ICB

Like it or not, your behavior is a powerful example to others. The question is not whether you will be an example to your friends; the only question is this: What kind of example will you be?

Corrie ten Boom advised, "Don't worry about what you do not understand. Worry about what you do understand in the Bible but do not live by." And that's good advice because your family and friends are always watching . . . and so, for that matter, is God.

A KID'S TIP

If you're a good example, everybody wins. If you're a bad example, everybody loses. So behave accordingly.

Actions speak louder than sermons . . . much louder.

Criswell Freeman

What does the Bible say about the way I should view my family?

THE QUICK ANSWER:

When you treat your family well, you're doing the right thing . . . and you're pleasing God.

Your Family Is a Gift

The first thing they need to learn is to do their duty to their own family. When they do this, they will be repaying their parents or grandparents. That pleases God.

1 Timothy 5:4 ICB

Your family is a wonderful, one-of-a-kind gift from God. And your family members love you very much—what a blessing it is to be loved!

Have you ever really stopped to think about how much you are loved?

Your parents love you (of course) and so does everybody else in your family. But it doesn't stop there. You're also an important part of God's family . . . and He loves you more than you can imagine.

What should you do about all the love that comes your way? You should accept it; you should be thankful for it; and you should share it . . . starting now!

A KID'S TIP

When something is bothering you, talk to your parents about it. Your parents will help you if you let them. Your job is to let them.

Live in the present and make the most of your opportunities to enjoy your family and friends.

Barbara Johnson

Sometimes it's hard for me to give things away, even if I don't use them anymore. Is it really important that I share things with other people?

THE QUICK ANSWER:

Yes. God wants you to be generous, cheerful, and kind.

Give Cheerfully and Often

God loves the person who gives happily.
2 Corinthians 9:7 ICB

Learning how to share can be an important way to build better self-esteem. Why? Because when you learn to share your things, you'll know that you've done exactly what God wants you to do—and you'll feel better about yourself.

The Bible teaches that it's better to be generous than selfish. But sometimes, you won't feel like sharing your things, and you'll be tempted to keep everything for yourself. When you're feeling a little bit stingy, remember this: God wants you to share your things with people who need your help.

When you learn to be a more generous person, God will be pleased with you . . . and you'll be pleased with yourself.

A KID'S TIP

Would you like to be a little happier? The Bible says that if you become a more generous person, you'll become a happier person, too.

The test of generosity is not how much you give, but how much you have left.

Anonymous

How should I treat my parents and grandparents?

THE QUICK ANSWER:
Respect them and treat them with the honor they deserve.

Respect Your Parents!

Honor your father and your mother.
Exodus 20:12 ICB

In the Ten Commandments, God makes it clear that you should be very good to your parents. So here's a question: are you the kind of obedient, helpful, respectful kid that you would want to take care of if you were a parent? Hopefully the answer to that question is a great big YES! After all, your parents love you more than you can imagine . . . and your parents work very hard to take care of you. So give your parents what they deserve: your respect.

A KID'S TIP

Calm down . . . sooner rather than later!
If you're angry with your mom or your
dad, don't blurt out something unkind.
If you can't say anything nice,
go to your room and don't come out
until you can.

How wonderful it is when parents
and children respect each other . . .
and show it.
Jim Gallery

Kids who know more
than their parents, don't.
Marie T. Freeman

Jesus loves me. What should I do in response to His love?

THE QUICK ANSWER:

You should love other people, just like Jesus loves you.

Jesus Loves Us and We Should Share His Love

Love other people just as Christ loved us.
Ephesians 5:2 ICB

The Bible makes it clear: Because Jesus loves you, you should love other people, too. But, of course, some folks are easier to love than others. Some folks are friendly, kind, and happy. And other folks aren't. But remember this: Jesus wants you to love all people, not just the loveable ones. That means that you should forgive everybody as quickly as possible. And while you're at it, you should remember that God wants you to love all people, today, tomorrow, and forever.

A KID'S TIP

It's good to tell your loved ones how you feel about them, but that's not enough. You should also show them how you feel with your good deeds and your kind words.

When you agree to let God love the unlovely through you, He never fails to make the unlovely lovely to you.

Beth Moore

How much a person loves someone is obvious by how much he is willing to sacrifice for that person.

Bill Bright

I'd like to make this world a better place. How can I live a life that really matters?

THE QUICK ANSWER:

Live the way that God wants you to live.

Be Wise: Obey God!

The Lord says, "I will make you wise and show you where to go. I will guide you and watch over you."

Psalm 32:8 NCV

If you look in a dictionary, you'll see that the word "wisdom" means "using good judgment, and knowing what is true." But there's more: it's not enough just to know what's right; if you really want to become a wise person, you must also do what's right.

A big part of "doing what's right" is learning to be obedient . . . and the best time to start being a more obedient person is right now! Why? Because it's the wise thing to do.

A KID'S TIP

Obeying God? Yes Sir! What about the rules you learn about in the Bible? Well, those aren't just any old rules— they're God's rules. And you should behave—and obey—accordingly.

You may not always see immediate results, but all God wants is your obedience and faithfulness.

Vonette Bright

We have not learned the commandments until we have learned to do them.

Vance Havner

When other people get into trouble, what should I do?

THE QUICK ANSWER:

The Bible wants us to offer help to people who need it.

When People Need Your Help

Help each other with your troubles.
When you do this, you truly obey
the law of Christ.

Galatians 6:2 ICB

Sometimes we would like to help make the world a better place, but we're not sure how to do it. Jesus told the story of the "Good Samaritan," a man who helped a fellow traveler when no one else would. We, too, should be good Samaritans when we find people who need our help. A good place to start helping other people is at home. And, of course, we should also offer our help at school and at church.

Another way that we can help other people is to pray for them. God always hears our prayers, so we should talk with Him as often as we can. When we do, we're not only doing a wonderful thing for the people we pray for, we're also doing a wonderful thing for ourselves, too. Why? Because we feel better about ourselves when we're helping other people. And the more we help others, the better we should feel about ourselves.

A KID'S TIP

Want to feel better about yourself? Find somebody to help. Ask yourself this question: "How helpful can I be?" When you help others, you'll be proud of yourself, and God will be, too!

How am I supposed to treat my neighbors?

THE QUICK ANSWER:

You should always be kind to your friends and neighbors.

Turning Neighbors Into Friends

This royal law is found in the Scriptures: "Love your neighbor as yourself." If you obey this law, then you are doing right.

James 2:8 ICB

The Bible tells us that friendship can be a wonderful thing. That's why it's good to know how to make and to keep good friends.

If you want to make lots of friends, practice the Golden Rule with everybody you know. Be kind. Share. Say nice things. Be helpful. When you do, you'll discover that the Golden Rule isn't just a nice way to behave; it's also a great way to make and to keep friends!

A KID'S TIP

If you want to make new friends, how can you do it? A good way to make friends—and a good way to keep them—is to become a better listener. Most people are happy to tell you about themselves, and they'll be even happier if you listen carefully. So learn to be a good listener—it's a good way to make new friends.

Yes, the Spirit was sent to be our Counselor. Yes, Jesus speaks to us personally. But often he works through another human being.

John Eldredge

Sometimes I am worried or scared. What can I do to be strong?

THE QUICK ANSWER:

You can talk to your parents, and you can talk to God. And that's exactly what you should do.

When in Doubt, Trust God

But the people who trust in the Lord will become strong again. They will rise up as an eagle in the sky. They will run without needing rest. They will walk without becoming tired.

Isaiah 40:31 ICB

If something scares you, tell your parents! Your parents love you and care for you, and they will protect you. And it's the same way with God. You can talk to Him about your problems, too. When you pray, God will listen. And

He's promised to protect you now and forever.

So if you're afraid or worried, there's always somebody you can talk to. You can talk to your parents, and you can talk to God. So don't keep things to yourself; start talking . . . now!

A KID'S TIP

If you have doubts, fears, or worries, talk things over with your parents. And be sure to talk to God, too. It's better to talk about troubles than it is to worry about them.

As God's children, we are the recipients of lavish love—a love that motivates us to keep trusting even when we have no idea what God is doing.

Beth Moore

Sometimes I'm tempted to follow my friends, even if they're misbehaving. What should I do?

THE QUICK ANSWER:

You should be much more concerned about pleasing God than pleasing your friends!

Try to Please God First

My dear friends, don't let public opinion influence how you live out our glorious, Christ-originated faith.

James 2:1 MSG

Are you a people-pleaser or a God-pleaser? Hopefully, you're far more concerned with pleasing God than you are with pleasing your friends. But face facts: even if you're a devoted Christian, you're still going to feel the urge to impress your friends—and sometimes that urge will be strong.

Here's your choice: you can choose to please God first, or you can fall victim to peer pressure. The choice is yours—and so are the consequences.

A KID'S TIP

Face facts: since you can't please everybody, you're better off trying to please the people who are trying to help you become a better person, not the people who are encouraging you to misbehave!

It is comfortable to know that we are responsible to God and not to man. It is a small matter to be judged of man's judgement.
Lottie Moon

Those who follow the crowd usually get lost in it.
Rick Warren

Does God forgive me when I am wrong?

THE QUICK ANSWER:

He forgives you just like you forgive others.

Be Quick to Forgive

Yes, if you forgive others for the things they do wrong, then your Father in heaven will also forgive you for the things you do wrong.
Matthew 6:14 ICB

How often does God forgive us? More times than we can count! And that, by the way, is exactly how many times that God expects us to forgive other people—more times than we care to count.

Of this you can be sure: God won't ever get tired of forgiving you. And, because He has forgiven you, He doesn't want you to get tired of forgiving other people . . . ever!

A KID'S TIP

The time to forgive is now! God wants you to forgive people now, not later. Why? Because God knows that it's the right thing to do. And, of course, God wants you to be happy, not angry. God knows what's best for you, so if you have somebody you need to forgive, do it now.

God calls upon the loved not just to love but to be loving. God calls upon the forgiven not just to forgive but to be forgiving.

Beth Moore

When is the best time to do the right thing?

THE QUICK ANSWER:

It's always the right time to do the right thing.

Do the Right Thing!

We must not become tired of doing good. We will receive our harvest of eternal life at the right time. We must not give up!

Galatians 6:9 ICB

If you're old enough to know right from wrong, then you're old enough to do something about it. In other words, you should always try to do the right thing, and you should also do your very best not to do the wrong thing.

The more self-control you have, the easier it is to do the right thing. Why?

Because, when you learn to think first and do things next, you avoid lots of silly mistakes. So here's great advice: first, slow down long enough to figure out the right thing to do—and then do it. You'll make yourself happy, and you'll make lots of other people happy, too.

A KID'S TIP

When you do the right thing, you don't have to worry about what you did or what you said. But, when you do the wrong thing, you'll be worried that someone will find out.
So do the right thing; it's the best—and the happiest—way to live.

Although God causes all things to work together for good for His children, He still holds us accountable for our behavior.

Kay Arthur

What is more important: how I look on the outside or how I am on the inside?

THE QUICK ANSWER:
God knows everything about you, and He sees your heart. And God cares about your heart, not the way you look.

Good Knows Your Heart

I am the Lord, and I can look into a person's heart.
Jeremiah 17:10 ICB

Other people see you from the outside, and sometimes people will judge you by the way you look. But God doesn't care how you look on the outside. Why? Because God is wiser than that; God cares about what you are on the inside— God sees your heart.

If you're like most people, you'll worry a little bit about the way you look (or maybe you'll worry a lot about it). But please don't worry too much about your appearance!

How you look on the outside isn't important . . . but how you feel on the inside is important. So don't worry about trying to impress other people. Instead of trying to impress other kids, try to impress God by being the best person you can be.

A KID'S TIP

Beauty on the outside isn't important . . . beauty on the inside is.

Outside appearances, things like the clothes you wear or the car you drive, are important to other people but totally unimportant to God. Trust God.

Marie T. Freeman

My parents tell me a lot of things. How carefully should I listen?

THE QUICK ANSWER:

The Bible says you should listen carefully to your parents. And you should obey them, too.

Be a Good Listener

My child, listen to your father's teaching. And do not forget your mother's advice.

Proverbs 1:8 ICB

Do you listen carefully to the things your parents tell you? You should. Your parents want the very best for you. They want you to be happy and healthy; they want you to be smart and to do smart things. Your parents have much to teach you, and you have much to learn. So listen carefully to the things your mom and dad have to say. And ask lots of questions. When you do, you'll soon discover that your parents have lots of answers . . . lots of very good answers.

A KID'S TIP

Since you love your family . . .
show it by behaving yourself
and obeying your family's rules!

Happiness is obedience,
and obedience is happiness.

C. H. Spurgeon

Obedience always enriches us.

Warren Wiersbe

Should I ever be afraid of the truth?

No. It's good to know the truth and tell the truth.

The Truth Makes Us Free

So Jesus said to the Jews who believed in him, "If you continue to obey my teaching, you are truly my followers. Then you will know the truth. And the truth will make you free."
John 8:31-32 ICB

Jesus had an important message for His followers. He said, "The truth will make you free." When we do the right thing and tell the truth, we don't need to worry about our lies catching up with us. When we behave honestly, we don't have to worry about feeling guilty or ashamed. But, if we fail to do what we know is right, bad things start to happen, and we feel guilty.

Jesus understood that the truth is a very good thing indeed. We should understand it, too. And we should keep telling it as long as we live.

A KID'S TIP

When you tell the truth and live by God's Truth, you'll be very glad you did!

The Holy Spirit is the Spirit of Truth, which means He always works according to and through the Word of God whether you feel Him or not.

Anne Graham Lotz

To worship Him in truth means to worship Him honestly, without hypocrisy, standing open and transparent before Him.

Anne Graham Lotz

What does the Bible say about love?

THE QUICK ANSWER:
The Bible says that it's important to be loving and kind.

Love Is Great

So these three things continue forever: faith, hope, and love. And the greatest of these is love.
1 Corinthians 13:13 ICB

In 1st Corinthians 13, God teaches us that love is important . . . very important! Faith is important, of course. And so is hope. But, love is more important still.

Jesus showed His love for us on the cross, and, as Christians, we are taught to return Christ's love by sharing it. So today, do yourself a big favor: Obey God's Word by sharing Christ's love with your family members and friends. And while you're at it, remember that it's not enough to tell people that you love them. You should also show them that you love them by being kind, courteous, and thoughtful.

A KID'S TIP

God loves you, and He wants you to share His love to those around you.

Forgiveness is the precondition of love.
Catherine Marshall

God is love, and He wants us to share that attribute with Him and with others.
Charles Stanley

It can be tempting to say bad things about other people. What does the Bible say about that?

THE QUICK ANSWER:

Don't gossip. And don't say anything behind a person's back that you wouldn't say to that person's face.

Don't Gossip

The things you say in the dark will be told in the light. The things you have whispered in an inner room will be shouted from the top of the house.

Luke 12:3 ICB

Do you know what gossip is? It's when we say bad things about people who are not around to hear us. When we say bad things about other people, we hurt them and we hurt ourselves. That's why the Bible tells us that gossip is wrong.

When we say things that we don't want other people to know we said, we're being somewhat dishonest, but if the things we say aren't true, we're being very dishonest. Either way, we have done something that we may regret later, especially if the other person finds out.

So do yourself a big favor: don't gossip. It's a waste of words, and it's the wrong thing to do. You'll feel better about yourself if you don't gossip about other people. So don't do it!

A KID'S TIP

Always watch what you say.
And don't say something behind
someone's back that you wouldn't
say to that person directly.

To belittle is to be little.

Anonymous

Can I say I love God if I hate some-body?

THE QUICK ANSWER:

The Bible says we can't hate another person and love God at the same time.

Hatred and Christianity Don't Mix

Anyone who claims to live in God's light and hates a brother or sister is still in the dark.

1 John 2:9 MSG

Face it: sometimes people can be cruel. And when people are unkind to you or to your friends, you may be tempted to strike back in anger. Don't do it! Instead, remember that God corrects other people's behaviors in His own way, and He doesn't need your help. So even when other people misbehave, God wants

you to forgive them . . . and that's what
you should do.

A KID'S TIP

How hard is it to love your enemies?
You'll never know until you try . . . so try!

Give me such love for God
and men as will blot out all
hatred and bitterness.
Dietrich Bonhoeffer

To hold on to hate and resentments
is to throw a monkey wrench
into the machinery of life.
E. Stanley Jones

Why is it important for me to behave myself like a Christian?

THE QUICK ANSWER:

Because people are watching you, and your example is important.

The Light of the World

You are the light that gives light to the world . . . Live so that they will see the good things you do. Live so that they will praise your Father in heaven.
Matthew 5:14, 16 ICB

Every Christian, each in his or her own way, has a responsibility to share the Good News of Jesus. And it's important to remember that we bear testimony through both words and actions. Wise Christians follow the advice of St. Francis of Assisi who advised, "Preach the gospel at all times and, if necessary, use words."

As you think about how your example influences others, remember that actions speak louder than words . . . much louder!

A KID'S TIP

The way that you behave yourself
is like a light that shines out upon
the world. Make sure that your light
is both bright and good.

Light is stronger than darkness—
darkness cannot "comprehend"
or "overcome" it.

Anne Graham Lotz

His life is our light—our purpose
and meaning and reason for living.

Anne Graham Lotz

This world is filled with things that can be hurtful. What does God want me to do about that?

THE QUICK ANSWER:
God wants you to guard your heart!

Guard Your Heart

Above all else, guard your heart, for it affects everything you do.
Proverbs 4:23 NLT

You are near and dear to God. He loves you more than you can imagine, and He wants the very best for you. And one more thing: God wants you to guard your heart.

Every day, you are faced with choices . . . lots of them. You can do the right thing, or not. You can tell the truth, or not. You can be kind and generous and obedient. Or not.

Your mind and your heart will usually tell you the right thing to do. And if you listen to your parents and grandparents, they will help you, too, by teaching you God's rules. Then, you will learn that doing the right thing is always better than doing the wrong thing. And, by obeying God's rules, you will guard your heart by giving it to His Son Jesus.

A KID'S TIP

God wants you to be careful about the things you watch, the things you think about, and the people you hang around with. Doing these things will help you guard your heart.

Nobody who gets enough food and clothing in a world where most are hungry and cold has any business to talk about "misery."

C. S. Lewis

I want to be happy. What do I need to do?

THE QUICK ANSWER:

Be wise, be humble, and be obedient to God.

Live Wisely and Happily

Are there those among you who are truly wise and understanding? Then they should show it by living right and doing good things with a gentleness that comes from wisdom.

James 3:13 NCV

Do you want to be happy? Here are some things you should do: Love God and His Son Jesus, obey the Golden Rule, and always try to do the right thing. When you do these things, you'll discover that happiness goes hand-in-hand with good behavior.

The happiest people do not misbehave; the happiest people are not cruel or greedy. The happiest people don't say unkind things. The happiest people are those who love God and follow His rules—starting, of course, with the Golden one.

A KID'S TIP

When you choose to do the right thing . . . you make everybody happy. You make your parents happy; you make your teachers happy; you make your friends happy; and you make God happy!

The more wisdom enters our hearts, the more we will be able to trust our hearts in difficult situations.

John Eldredge

What is the best thing I can do for the people who are mean to me?

THE QUICK ANSWER:
Pray for them, forgive them, and be as kind to them as possible.

When People Aren't Nice

I tell you, love your enemies.
Pray for those who hurt you.
If you do this, you will be true sons
of your Father in heaven.
Matthew 6:44-45 ICB

Sometimes people can be rude . . . very rude. As long as you live, you will face countless opportunities to lose your temper when other folks behave badly. But God has a better plan: He wants you to forgive people and move on. Remember that God has already forgiven you, so it's only right that you should be willing to forgive others.

So here's some good advice: Forgive everybody as quickly as you can, and leave the rest up to God.

A KID'S TIP

Sometimes people can be difficult,
and sometimes friends misbehave.
But it doesn't pay to get angry—your job
is to be as understanding as possible.
And while you're at it, remember that
God wants you to forgive other folks,
just like He forgives you.

We are all fallen creatures
and all very hard to live with.

C. S. Lewis

You don't have to attend every argument
you're invited to!

Anonymous

What will happen if I study the Bible and obey God's teachings?

THE QUICK ANSWER:
If you learn God's rules and obey them, you'll be happier.

Obey God Today . . . and Every Day!

But the truly happy person is the one who carefully studies God's perfect law that makes people free. He continues to study it. He listens to God's teaching and does not forget what he heard. Then he obeys what God's teaching says.

James 1:25 ICB

How can you show God how much you love Him? By obeying His commandments, that's how! When you follow God's rules, you show Him that you have real respect for Him and for His Son.

Sometimes, you will be tempted to disobey God, but don't do it. And sometimes you'll be tempted to disobey your parents or your teachers . . . but don't do that, either.

When your parent steps away or a teacher looks away, it's up to you to control yourself. And of this you can be sure: If you really want to control yourself, you can do it!

A KID'S TIP

When should you get tired of obeying God? The answer to that question is simple: Never!

We learn to determine the will of God by working at it. The more we obey, the easier it is to discover what God wants us to do.

Warren Wiersbe

Should I be afraid to ask God for the things I need?

THE QUICK ANSWER:

The Bible instructs us to ask God for the things we need. So don't hesitate to ask God to help you and lead you.

Ask God!

Continue to ask, and God will give to you. Continue to search, and you will find. Continue to knock, and the door will open for you.

Matthew 7:7 ICB

What should you do if you need something? Well, of course you can ask your parents, but you shouldn't stop there. You can also ask for God's help, too.

The Bible makes it clear that when you need help, you can always ask God.

And you shouldn't just ask Him one time. You should keep asking for His help. And while you're at it, you should do your fair share of the work, trusting that when you've done your best, it's up to God to do the rest.

A KID'S TIP

Pray early and often. One way to make sure that your heart is in tune with God is to pray often. The more you talk to God, the more He will talk to you.

Some people think God does not like to be troubled with our constant asking. But, the way to trouble God is not to come at all.

D. L. Moody

God uses our most stumbling, faltering faith-steps as the open door to His doing for us "more than we ask or think."

Catherine Marshall

How important is it for me to pray every day?

THE QUICK ANSWER:

The Bible teaches us that it's very important to pray. God wants us to pray, He hears our prayers, and He answers our prayers in His own way.

God Hears Your Prayers and Answers

Do not worry about anything. But pray and ask God for everything you need.
Philippians 4:6 ICB

In case you've been wondering, wonder no more—God does answer your prayers. What God does not do is this: He does not always answer your prayers as soon as you might like, and He does not always answer your prayers by saying "Yes."

God answers prayers not only according to our wishes but also according to His master plan. And guess what? We don't know that plan . . . but we can know the Planner.

Are you praying? Then you can be sure that God is listening. And sometime soon, He'll answer!

A KID'S TIP

Open-eyed prayers: When you are praying, your eyes don't always have to be closed. Of course it's good to close your eyes and bow your head, but you can also offer a quick prayer to God with your eyes open. That means that you can pray anytime you want.

Prayer moves the arm that moves the world.

Annie Armstrong

How can I be happy?

THE QUICK ANSWER:

If you obey God's commandments and think good thoughts, you'll be a happier person.

How to Be Happy

How happy are those whose way is blameless, who live according to the law of the Lord! Happy are those who keep His decrees and seek Him with all their heart.

Psalm 119:1-2 HCSB

If we could decide to be happy "once and for all," life would be so much simpler, but it doesn't seem to work that way. If we want happiness to last, we need to create good thoughts every day that we live. Yesterday's good thoughts aren't enough . . . we've got to think more good thoughts today.

Each new day is a gift from God, so treat it that way. Think about it like this: today is another wonderful chance to celebrate God's gifts.

So celebrate—starting now—and keep celebrating forever!

A KID'S TIP

The best day to be happy is this one. Don't spend your whole life in the waiting room. Make up your mind to celebrate today.

I became aware of one very important concept I had missed before:
my attitude—not my circumstances—
was what was making me unhappy.

Vonette Bright

It seems to me that happiness is not the major goal of life, but instead is a wonderful by-product.

Warren Wiersbe

I know it's important to encourage other people. How can I be encouraging to my family and friends?

THE QUICK ANSWER:
Be good and say encouraging words.

Encouraging Others

*A good person's words
will help many others.*
Proverbs 10:21 ICB

When other people are sad, what can we do? We can do our best to cheer them up by showing kindness and love.

The Bible tells us that we must care for each other, and when everybody is happy, that's an easy thing to do. But, when people are sad, for whatever reason, it's up to us to speak a kind word or to offer a helping hand.

Do you know someone who is discouraged or sad? If so, perhaps it's time to take matters into your own hands. Think of something you can do to cheer that person up . . . and then do it! You'll make two people happy.

A KID'S TIP

If you want to cheer someone up but can't think of something to say or do, try drawing a picture or writing a note.

How many people stop because so few say, "Go!"

Charles Swindoll

One of the best ways to encourage someone who's hurting is with your ears—by listening.

Barbara Johnson

Sometimes I have a bad attitude. What does the Bible say about that?

THE QUICK ANSWER:

The Bible says it's better to be cheerful than to be angry.

A Continual Feast

A cheerful heart has a continual feast.

Proverbs 15:15 HCSB

What is a continual feast? It's a little bit like a non-stop birthday party: fun, fun, and more fun! The Bible tells us that a cheerful heart can make life like a continual feast, and that's something worth working for.

Where does cheerfulness begin? It begins inside each of us; it begins in the heart. So today and every day, let's be thankful to God for His blessings, and let's show our thanks by sharing good cheer wherever we go. This old world needs all the cheering up it can get . . . and so do we!

A KID'S TIP

God has given you many blessings, and you have many reasons to be cheerful. So what are you waiting for?

The people whom I have seen succeed best in life have always been cheerful and hopeful people who went about their business with a smile on their faces.

Charles Kingsley

Sour godliness is the devil's religion.

John Wesley

Everyday I have a lot of decisions to make. How do I know I'm making the right ones?

THE QUICK ANSWER:

Always try to make choices that are pleasing to God.

Making Good Choices

The Lord says, "I will make you wise
and show you where to go.
I will guide you and watch over you."
Psalm 32:8 NCV

Your life is a series of choices. From the instant you wake up in the morning until the moment you nod off to sleep at night, you make lots of decisions: decisions about the things you do, decisions about the words you speak, and decisions about the thoughts you choose to think.

So, if you want to lead a life that is pleasing to God, you must make choices that are pleasing to Him. And you know what? He deserves no less . . . and neither, for that matter, do you.

A KID'S TIP

Think before you say things . . . and think before you do things. Otherwise, you can get yourself in trouble. So here's a good rule to follow: Slow down long enough to think about the things you're about to do or say. That way, you'll make better choices.

When we learn to listen to Christ's voice for the details of our daily decisions, we begin to know Him personally.

Catherine Marshall

God always gives His best to those who leave the choice with Him.

Jim Elliot

If I say unkind things, I hurt myself. What happens when I speak kind words?

THE QUICK ANSWER:
When you speak kind words, you'll make everybody happy.

Kind Words Are Wonderful

Pleasant words are like a honeycomb. They make a person happy and healthy.
Proverbs 16:24 ICB

Have you learned to control the words you speak? Hopefully so. After all, your words have the power to help other people. And, since you want other folks to say kind things to you, you should say kind things to them, too.

So make certain that you're a person who says helpful things, not hurtful things. You'll feel better about yourself when you help other people feel better about themselves. Everybody needs to hear kind words, and that's exactly the kind of words they should hear from you!

A KID'S TIP

If you don't know what to say . . . don't say anything. Sometimes, a hug works better than a whole mouthful of words.

When you talk, choose the very same
words that you would use if
Jesus were looking over your shoulder.
Because He is.
Marie T. Freeman

Fill the heart with the love of Christ
so that only truth and purity
can come out of the mouth.
Warren Wiersbe

Can I be a happy Christian?

THE QUICK ANSWER:

Yes! Being a Christian can (and should) be a joyful experience. So celebrate!

Let's Celebrate

*Celebrate God all day, every day.
I mean, revel in him!*
Philippians 4:4 MSG

Today is a day of celebration, and hopefully, you do feel like celebrating! After all, today (like every other day) should be a special time to thank God for all the wonderful things He has given you.

So don't wait for birthdays or holidays—make every day a special day, including this one. Take time to pause and thank God for His gifts. He deserves your thanks, and you deserve to celebrate!

A KID'S TIP

If you don't feel like celebrating,
start counting your blessings.
Before long, you'll realize that you
have plenty of reasons to celebrate.

If you can forgive the person
you were, accept the person you are,
and believe in the person you will
become, you are headed for joy.
So celebrate your life.

Barbara Johnson

I am truly happy with Jesus Christ.
I couldn't live without Him.

Ruth Bell Graham

How can I show that I'm a good person?

THE QUICK ANSWER:

By behaving yourself and doing what is right.

Your Behavior Speaks for Itself

Even a child is known by his behavior. His actions show if he is innocent and good.

Proverbs 20:11 ICB

Do you behave differently because you're a Christian? Or do you behave in pretty much the same way that you would if you had never heard of Jesus? Hopefully, your behavior is better because of the things you've learned from the Bible.

Doing the right thing is not always easy, especially when you're tired or frustrated. But, doing the wrong thing almost always leads to trouble. So here's some advice: remember the lessons you learn from the Bible. And keep remembering them every day of your life.

A KID'S TIP

If you're not sure that it's the right thing to do, don't do it! And if you're not sure that it's the truth, don't tell it.

The best evidence of our having the truth is our walking in the truth.
Matthew Henry

Never support an experience which does not have God as its source and faith in God as its result.
Oswald Chambers

God has a plan for me. How can I figure it out?

You should pray about God's plan for your life. And while you're at it, you should keep your eyes and heart open for any messages that God may send your way.

Father Knows Best!

The thing you should want most is God's kingdom and doing what God wants. Then all these other things you need will be given to you.

Matthew 6:33 ICB

God has a plan for you. But God's plan may not always happen in the way that you would like or at the time of your own choosing. Still, God always knows best.

Sometimes, even though you may want something very badly, you must still be patient and wait for the right time to get it, And the right time, of course, is determined by God. So trust Him always, obey Him always, and wait for Him to show you His plans. And that's exactly what He will do.

A KID'S TIP

God has very big plans in store for your life, so trust Him and wait patiently for those plans to unfold. And remember: God's timing is best.

Letting God have His way can be an uncomfortable thing.

Charles Swindoll

God cannot lead the individual who is not willing to give Him a blank check with his life.

Catherine Marshall

I've heard of the Golden Rule, but what does it really mean?

THE QUICK ANSWER:

Treat others the same way you want to be treated by them.

The Rule That's Golden

Do for other people the same things you want them to do for you.

Matthew 7:12 ICB

How should you treat other people? Jesus has the answer to that question. Jesus wants you to treat other people exactly like you want to be treated: with kindness, respect, and courtesy. When you do, you'll make your family and friends happy . . . and that's what God wants.

So if you're wondering how to treat someone else, follow the Golden Rule:

treat the other people like you want them to treat you. When you do, you'll be obeying your Father in heaven and you'll be making other folks happy at the same time.

A KID'S TIP

If you want others to treat you according to the Golden Rule, then you should be quick to treat them in the same way. In other words, always play by the rule: the Golden Rule.

The Golden Rule starts at home, but it should never stop there.

Marie T. Freeman

It is one of the most beautiful compensations of life that no one can sincerely try to help another without helping herself.

Barbara Johnson

Why is God's Word so important to read and know?

THE QUICK ANSWER:

The Bible teaches you how to live, how to worship, and how to have eternal life.

God's Holy Word Is the Final Word

All Scripture is inspired by God and is profitable for teaching, for rebuking, for correcting, for training in righteousness, so that the man of God may be complete, equipped for every good work.

2 Timothy 3:16-17 HCSB

If you want to know God, you should read the book He wrote. It's called the Bible (of course!), and God uses it to teach you and guide you. The Bible is not like any other book. It is an amazing gift from your Heavenly Father.

D. L. Moody observed, "The Bible was not given to increase our knowledge but to change our lives." God's Holy Word is, indeed, a life-changing, one-of-a-kind treasure. Handle it with care, but more importantly, handle it every day!

A KID'S TIP

Read the Bible? Every day!
Try to read your Bible with
your parents every day.
If they forget, remind them!

There is no way to draw closer to God unless you are in the Word of God every day. It's your compass. Your guide. You can't get where you need to go without it.

Stormie Omartian

I've been tempted to take things that aren't mine. How can I make sure I do the right thing?

THE QUICK ANSWER:
Always look to God and stay focused on Him. Always try to please God.

If It Isn't Yours, Don't Take It!

Keep your eyes focused on what is right.
Keep looking straight ahead
to what is good.
Proverbs 4:25 ICB

The Bible makes it clear: you should never take things that don't belong to you. So if you're ever tempted to take something that isn't yours, stop before you take it, and think about the consequences.

Here's something that you're bound to learn sooner or later, so you might as well learn it right now: When you do the right thing, you'll feel better about yourself, and you'll be happier.

So, if you want to feel better about yourself, do yourself a favor: tell the truth, and never take things that don't belong to you. When you do, you'll discover that honesty is, indeed, the best policy.

A KID'S TIP

Sometimes, the best way to control yourself is to slow yourself down. Then, you can think about the things you're about to do before you do them.

The only power the devil has is in getting people to believe his lies. If they don't believe his lies, he is powerless to get his work done.

Stormie Omartian

Today is another day. Why should I be glad about that?

THE QUICK ANSWER:

Every day is a gift from God. So celebrate!

Be Joyful!

This is the day that the LORD has made. Let us rejoice and be glad today!
Psalm 118:24 ICB

Are you one of those kids who has made the choice to rejoice? Hopefully so. After all, if you're a Christian, you have plenty of reasons to be joyful.

So today, think about this: God has given you too many blessings to count, but you can certainly count some of those blessings. Your job is to honor God with your prayers, your words, your behavior, and your joy.

A KID'S TIP

Want to be joyful?
Think good thoughts, do good deeds,
make good friends, and obey God.
When you do these things,
you'll never be sad for long.

The joy of the Holy Spirit is
experienced by giving thanks
in all situations.

Bill Bright

According to Jesus, it is God's will
that His children be filled
with the joy of life.

Catherine Marshall

How does God go about persuading people to love Him?

He uses good people like you to tell others about His Son.

Share the Good News!

We're Christ's representatives. God uses us to persuade men and women to drop their differences and enter into God's work of making things right between them. We're speaking for Christ himself now: Become friends with God; he's already a friend with you.

2 Corinthians 5:20 MSG

We live in a world that desperately needs the healing message of Christ Jesus. Every believer, each in his or her own way, bears responsibility for sharing the Good News of our Savior.

It is important to remember that we bear testimony through both words and actions.

Now is the time to share your testimony with others. So today, preach the Gospel through your words and your deeds . . . but not necessarily in that order.

A KID'S TIP

Don't be afraid to talk about Jesus. And remember, you're never too young to tell somebody else about God.

Your light is the truth of the Gospel message itself as well as your witness as to Who Jesus is and what He has done for you. Don't hide it.

Anne Graham Lotz

Does God want me to talk to Him every day?

THE QUICK ANSWER:

Yes, God wants you to pray every day. And He wants you to study the Bible, too.

Starting Your Day with God

Morning by morning he wakens me and opens my understanding to his will. The Sovereign Lord has spoken to me, and I have listened.

Isaiah 50:4-5 NLT

How do you start your day? Do you sleep till the last possible moment and then hop out of bed without giving a single thought to God? Hopefully not. If you're smart, you'll start your day with a prayer of thanks to your Heavenly Father.

Each new day is a gift from God, and if you're wise, you'll spend a few quiet moments thanking the Giver. It's a wonderful way to start your day.

A KID'S TIP

Do you have a special place where you and your parents read daily devotionals? If not, you should ask your mom or dad to help you think of a good place where the two of you can read the Bible and talk to God.

A child of God should never leave his bedroom in the morning without being on good terms with God.

C. H. Spurgeon

When you meet with God, open the Bible. Don't rely on your memory; rely on those printed pages.

Charles Swindoll

If I make mistakes, will God ever give up on me?

THE QUICK ANSWER:
God will never leave you, not even for a moment. And when you make a mistake, God will forgive you if you ask Him to.

God Loves You and Forgives You

God, who got you started in this spiritual adventure, shares with us the life of his Son and our Master Jesus. He will never give up on you.
1 Corinthians 1:9 MSG

Are you perfect? Of course not! Even if you're a very good person, you're bound to mistakes and lots of them.

When you make a mistake, you must try your best to learn from it (so that you won't make the very same mistake

again). And, if you have hurt someone—
or if you have disobeyed God—you
must ask for forgiveness. And here's
the good news: when you ask for God's
forgiveness, He will always give it. God
forgives you every single time you ask
Him to. So ask!

A KID'S TIP

God loves you more than you can
imagine, and He's prepared a place
for you in heaven. So celebrate
God's love today and every day.

God soon turns from his wrath,
but he never turns from his love.

C. H. Spurgeon

There is no pit so deep that
God's love is not deeper still.

Corrie ten Boom

There are so many things I want. Should I be more interested in getting these things, or should I be more concerned about the things I give to other people?

THE QUICK ANSWER:
According to the Bible, giving is better than getting.

It's Good to Give

Remember the words of Jesus. He said, "It is more blessed to give than to receive."
Acts 20:35 ICB

Jesus said that it's better to give than to receive. That means that we should be generous with other people—but sometimes we don't feel much like sharing. Instead of sharing the things that we have, we want to keep them all to ourselves. That's when we must remember that God doesn't want selfishness to rule our hearts; He wants us to be generous.

Are you lucky enough to have nice things? If so, God's instructions are clear: you must share your blessings with others. And that's exactly the way it should be. After all, think how generous God has been with you.

A KID'S TIP

When are you old enough to start giving? If you're old enough to understand these words, you're old enough to start giving to your church and to those who are less fortunate than you. If you're not sure about the best way to do it, ask your parents!

Nothing is really ours until we share it.

C. S. Lewis

When I decide to follow Jesus, what happens?

THE QUICK ANSWER:

Your life will be changed forever ... and you will walk in His eternal light.

Following Jesus into the Light

I have come as light into the world so that whoever believes in me would not stay in darkness.

John 12:46 NCV

Jesus wants to have a real relationship with you. Are you willing to have a real relationship with Him? Unless you can answer this question with a resounding "Yes," you may miss out on some wonderful things.

This day offers yet another opportunity to behave yourself like a real Christian by following Jesus into the light. When you do, God will guide your steps and bless your endeavors . . . forever.

A KID'S TIP

What a friend you have in Jesus:
Jesus loves you, and He offers you
eternal life with Him in heaven.
Welcome Him into your heart. Now!

I am truly happy with Jesus Christ.
I couldn't live without Him.
When my life gets beyond the ability
to cope, He takes over.

Ruth Bell Graham

The key to my understanding of
the Bible is a personal relationship
to Jesus Christ.

Oswald Chambers

When one of my friends is unkind, what should I do?

THE QUICK ANSWER:

When a friend makes a mistake, forgive him or her as quickly as you can.

When Forgiveness Is Hard

Hatred stirs up trouble,
but love forgives all wrongs.
Proverbs 10:12 NCV

Is forgiving someone else an easy thing for you to do or a hard thing? If you're like most people, forgiving others can be hard, Hard, HARD! But even if you're having a very hard time forgiving someone, you can do it if you talk things over with your parents, and if you talk things over with God.

Do you find forgiveness difficult? Talk about it and pray about it. You'll feel better when you do.

A KID'S TIP

Forgiving other people is a good way to make yourself feel better. Why? First, when you forgive others, you know that you're obeying God, and that's a good feeling. Second, forgiveness is a great way to stop feeling angry— and that's a good feeling, too!

In friendship, God opens your eyes to the glories of Himself.

Joni Eareckson Tada

A friend is one who makes me do my best.

Oswald Chambers

How can I have the best life I could ever dream of?

THE QUICK ANSWER:

Trust Jesus and let Him rule over your heart. When you do, you will have a wonderful life.

Your Wonderful Life with Jesus

I have come that they may have life, and that they may have it more abundantly.
John 10:10 NKJV

God has big plans for you, plans that include many good things. But God probably won't hand everything to you on a silver platter. He expects you to do your part to make His plans come true. That means that you'll need to become the kind of person that God—and your parents—want you to be.

So remember this: Your life is a glorious opportunity. Your job is to do what's right and obey God. When you do, good things will happen . . . lots of good things.

A KID'S TIP

Count your blessings . . . if you can! If you need a little cheering up, start counting your blessings. In truth, you really have too many blessings to count, but it never hurts to try.

Yes, we were created for His holy pleasure, but we will ultimately— if not immediately—find much pleasure in His pleasure.

Beth Moore

If we were given all we wanted here, our hearts would settle for this world rather than the next.

Elisabeth Elliot

When I know I have done something wrong, how can I make it right with God?

THE QUICK ANSWER:
Tell Him you are sorry.

Fix Your Mistakes and Say You're Sorry

*If we confess our sins,
He is faithful and righteous to forgive
us our sins and to cleanse us from
all unrighteousness.*
1 John 1:9 HCSB

Mistakes: nobody likes 'em but everybody makes 'em. And you're no different! When you make mistakes (and you will), you should do your best to correct them, to learn from them, and pray for the wisdom to avoid those same mistakes in the future.

If you want to become smarter faster, you'll learn from your mistakes the first time you make them. When you do, that means that you won't keep making the same mistakes over and over again, and that's the smart way to live.

A KID'S TIP

When you make a mistake, learn something . . . and forgive someone: yourself. Remember, you don't have to be perfect to be wonderful.

Father, take our mistakes
and turn them into opportunities.

Max Lucado

God is able to take mistakes, when they are committed to Him, and make of them something for our good and for His glory.

Ruth Bell Graham

What should I do if I have extra clothes, food, or toys?

THE QUICK ANSWER:

You should share your extra clothes, food, and toys, especially with the needy.

The Joys of Giving

If you have two shirts, share with the person who does not have one. If you have food, share that too.

Luke 3:11 ICB

Are you one of those kids who is lucky enough to have a closet filled up with stuff? If so, it's probably time to share some of it.

When your mom or dad says it's time to clean up your closet and give some things away, don't be sad. Instead of whining, think about all the children who could enjoy the things that you don't use very much. And while you're at it, think about what Jesus might tell you to do if He were here. Jesus would tell you to share generously and cheerfully. And that's exactly what you should do!

A KID'S TIP

Find loving homes for clothes and toys: Your parents can help you find younger children who need the clothes and toys that you've outgrown.

But the proper aim of giving is to put the recipient in a state where he no longer needs our gift.

C. S. Lewis

Selfishness is as far from Christianity as darkness is from light.

C. H. Spurgeon

What does God want me to do about His Son Jesus?

THE QUICK ANSWER:
God asks you to believe in His Son, Jesus.

The Promise of Eternal Life

Most assuredly, I say to you, he who believes in Me has everlasting life.
John 6:47 NKJV

It's time to remind yourself of a promise that God made a long time ago—the promise that God sent His Son Jesus to save the world and to save you! When you believe in Jesus, you will have eternal life. And when you stop to think about it, there can be no greater promise than that.

No matter where you are, God is with you. God loves you, and He sent His Son so that you can live forever in heaven with your loved ones. WOW! That's the greatest promise in the history of the universe. The End.

A KID'S TIP

Heaven is all those wonderful things
you wish you had on earth . . .
and so very much more.

God loves you and wants you to
experience peace and life—
abundant and eternal.

Billy Graham

Once a man is united to God,
how could he not live forever?
Once a man is separated from God,
what can he do but wither and die?

C. S. Lewis

Why is it that I don't always get what I want when I want it?

THE QUICK ANSWER:
God is in charge of giving us what we need when we need it.

God's Plan Is Best

He told them,
"You don't get to know the time.
Timing is the Father's business."
Acts 1:7 MSG

Sometimes, things happen that we simply don't understand. Sometimes we don't get what we want when we want it. And that's exactly how God intends it! You see God has given us many gifts, but He hasn't given us the power to understand everything that happens in our world (that comes later, when we get to heaven).

The Bible tells us God's plans are far bigger than we humans can possibly understand. That's one of the reasons that God doesn't make His plans clear to us. But even when we can't understand why God allows certain things to happen, we can trust His love for us.

The Bible does make one part of God's plan perfectly clear: we should accept His Son Jesus into our hearts so that we might have eternal life. And when we do, we are protected today, tomorrow, and forever.

A KID'S TIP

You should always trust God, and you should wait patiently for His plans to unfold. God's timing is best.

Waiting on God brings us to the journey's end quicker than our feet.

Mrs. Charles E. Cowman

How can I be sure that my future will be bright?

THE QUICK ANSWER:

Because Jesus lives. And when you follow Him, your future is eternally bright.

Your Very Bright Future

What a God we have! And how fortunate we are to have him, this Father of our Master Jesus! Because Jesus was raised from the dead, we've been given a brand-new life and have everything to live for, including a future in heaven— and the future starts now!

1 Peter 1:3-4 MSG

How bright is your future? Well, if you're a faithful believer, God's plans for you are so bright that you'd better wear shades. But here's an important question: How bright do you believe your future to be? Are you expecting a terrific tomorrow, or are you dreading a terrible one? The answer you give will have a powerful impact on the way tomorrow turns out.

So today, as you live in the present and look to the future, remember that God has an amazing plan for you. Act—and believe—accordingly.

A KID'S TIP

If you follow in Christ's footsteps, your future is amazingly bright. So don't delay—follow Jesus today!

Like little children on Christmas Eve, we know that lovely surprises are in the making. We can't see them. We have simply been told, and we believe. Tomorrow we shall see.

Elisabeth Elliot

Sometimes, God allows things to happen that I just don't understand. What does the Bible say about trusting God?

THE QUICK ANSWER:
The Bible teaches you to trust God with all your heart.

Trust God

Trust the Lord with all your heart.
Don't depend on your own
understanding. Remember the Lord
in everything you do.
And he will give you success.

Proverbs 3:5-6 ICB

How can you get to know God if you're unwilling to trust Him? The answer, of course, is that you can't. That's why you should trust God to handle everything, including your worries, your challenges, and your future.

God has big plans for you. And He has promised to protect you now and throughout eternity. So trust Him today, tomorrow, and always.

A KID'S TIP

The more you trust God, the less you'll worry about the things that bother other kids. So learn to trust God more—and worry less!

Ten thousand enemies cannot stop a Christian, cannot even slow him down, if he meets them in an attitude of complete trust in God.

A. W. Tozer

Our only means of living in Him is by faith, so trusting Him to see us through any and all trials and testings delights our Lord!

Bill Bright

There are a lot of things to read and watch. What does the Bible say about the things that I watch and read?

THE QUICK ANSWER:

The Bible teaches you to fill your mind with good thoughts.

Think Good Thoughts

Finally brothers, whatever is true, whatever is honorable, whatever is just, whatever is pure, whatever is lovely, whatever is commendable—if there is any moral excellence and if there is any praise—dwell on these things.

Philippians 4:8 HCSB

A joyful life starts with a joyful attitude. So when you're feeling a little tired or sad, here's something to remember: This day is a gift from God. And it's up to you to enjoy this day by trying to be cheerful, helpful, courteous, and well behaved. How can you do these things? A good place to start is by doing your best to think good thoughts.

God wants you to have a happy, joyful life, but that doesn't mean that you'll be happy all the time. Sometimes, you won't feel like feeling happy, and when you don't, you should talk to your parents about your emotions. When you talk things over with your parents, you'll feel better . . . and they'll feel better, too.

A KID'S TIP

Good thoughts lead to good deeds and bad thoughts lead elsewhere. So guard your thoughts accordingly.

It is the thoughts and intents of the heart that shape a person's life.

John Eldredge

If I love God (and myself) how should I treat my body?

THE QUICK ANSWER:

You should appreciate the body God gave you, and live purely.

Take Care of Your Body!

And so, dear brothers and sisters, I plead with you to give your bodies to God. Let them be a living and holy sacrifice—the kind he will accept. When you think of what he has done for you, is this too much to ask?

Romans 12:1 NLT

The Bible has clear instructions about taking care of yourself. You see, God gave you a wonderful, amazing, one-of-a-kind body, and He expects you to take good care of it. In fact, the Bible describes your body as a "temple"—a very important place that is near and dear to the heart of God.

So it's important to start forming healthy habits when you're young. And it's always smart to think about safety by doing things like buckling up every time you ride in a car. After all, your body is a precious gift from God, and He wants you to protect it. So be health-conscious and safety-conscious. Always!

A KID'S TIP

Your body is a priceless gift from God: handle with care!

God wants you to give Him your body. Some people do foolish things with their bodies. God wants your body as a holy sacrifice.

Warren Wiersbe

Where does real peace come from?

THE QUICK ANSWER:

Real peace comes from Jesus. If you want to be peaceful, happy, and wise, give your heart to Christ.

Jesus Offers Peace

I leave you peace.
My peace I give you. I do not give
it to you as the world does.
So don't let your hearts be troubled.
John 14:27 ICB

The beautiful words of John 14:27 remind us that Jesus offers us peace, not as the world gives, but as He alone gives. We, as believers, can accept His peace or ignore it. When we accept the peace of Jesus Christ into our hearts, our lives are changed forever, and we become more loving, patient Christians.

Christ's peace is offered freely; it has already been paid for; it is ours for the asking. So let us ask . . . and then share.

A KID'S TIP

God's peace can be yours right now. . . if you open up your heart and invite Him in.

Prayer guards hearts and minds and causes God to bring peace out of chaos.
Beth Moore

The more closely you cling to the Lord Jesus, the more clear will your peace be.
C. H. Spurgeon

Even though I am young, can God use me to help others?

THE QUICK ANSWER:

Yes, God uses people of all ages. So keep your eyes open for ways you can share Christ's Good News.

Talk About Your Faith

Get the word out. Teach all these things. And don't let anyone put you down because you're young. Teach believers with your life: by word, by demeanor, by love, by faith, by integrity.
1 Timothy 4:11-12 MSG

A good way to build your faith is by talking about it—to friends and family members—and that's precisely what God wants you to do.

In his second letter to Timothy, Paul shares a message to believers of every generation when he writes, "God has not given us a spirit of timidity" (1:7). Paul's meaning is crystal clear: When sharing our testimonies, we should be courageous and unashamed.

A KID'S TIP

It's important to tell the truth . . . and it's important to tell people about God's Truth (with a capital T).

There is nothing more appealing or convincing to a watching world than to hear the testimony of someone who has just been with Jesus.

Henry Blackaby

Claim the joy that is yours. Pray. And know that your joy is used by God to reach others.

Kay Arthur

How important is it to be honest?

THE QUICK ANSWER:

The Bible says that being dishonest can cause you a lot of problems.

It's Important
to Be Honest

*Dishonesty will destroy those
who are not trustworthy.*
Proverbs 11:3 ICB

It's important to be honest. When you tell the truth, you'll feel better about yourself, and other people will feel better about you, too. But that's not all. When you tell the truth, God knows—and He will reward you for your honesty.

Telling the truth is hard sometimes. But it's better to be honest, even when it's hard. So remember this: telling the truth is always the right thing to do . . . always.

A KID'S TIP

Sometimes, it's better to say nothing.
If you're tempted to say something
that isn't true, don't say anything.
A closed mouth tells no lies.

God doesn't expect you
to be perfect, but he does insist
on complete honesty.

Rick Warren

A lie is like a snowball:
the further you roll it,
the bigger it becomes.

Martin Luther

If my teacher or my parents correct me, what should I do?

THE QUICK ANSWER:

Listen carefully to the things that adults are trying to teach you. You can learn many things from the adults who care about you.

When Your Parents Correct You

A wise person pays attention to correction that will improve his life.
Proverbs 15:31 ICB

Sometimes you make mistakes, and your parents correct you. And sometimes, your teachers may correct you, too. Whenever a parent, grandparent, teacher, or coach offers you advice, you can either listen to it carefully or ignore it completely. The choice is yours.

If you're wise, you'll try to learn something every single time you're corrected. And the better you listen, the faster you'll learn.

A KID'S TIP

Why do your parents correct you? Because they love you . . . and because they want you to learn. So if your parents are kind enough to offer you correction, listen and learn.

If one examines the secret behind a championship football team, a magnificent orchestra, or a successful business, the principal ingredient is invariably discipline.

James Dobson

The alternative to discipline is disaster.

Vance Havner

I'd like to be popular with my friends, but sometimes they do things I don't approve of. What should I do?

THE QUICK ANSWER:

Be kind to everybody, but don't try to please everybody—try to please God (and, of course, your parents). And if one of your friends wants you to mis-behave, don't do it!

Please God

Obviously, I'm not trying to be a people pleaser! No, I am trying to please God. If I were still trying to please people, I would not be Christ's servant.

Galatians 1:10 NLT

Are you one of those people who tries to please everybody in sight? If so, you'd better watch out! After all, if you worry too much about pleasing your friends, you may not worry enough about pleasing God.

Whom will you try to please today: your God or your pals? The answer to that question should be simple. Your first job is to obey God's rules . . . and that means obeying your parents, too!

So don't worry too much about pleasing your friends or neighbors. Try, instead, to please your heavenly Father and your parents. No exceptions.

A KID'S TIP

You simply cannot please everybody.
So here's what you should do:
Try pleasing God and your parents.

Don't be addicted to approval.
Follow your heart. Do what you believe
God is telling you to do, and stand firm
in Him and Him alone.
Joyce Meyer

I want Jesus to be proud of me. How can I do that?

THE QUICK ANSWER:

Obey His commandments and honor His name.

Honor Jesus and Walk with Him

If your life honors the name of Jesus, he will honor you.

2 Thessalonians 1:12 MSG

Who will you walk with today? Do yourself a favor—walk with Jesus!

God's Word promises that when you follow in Christ's footsteps, you will learn how to behave yourself, and you'll learn how to live a good life. Jesus wants you to be a "new creation" through Him. And that's exactly what you should want for yourself, too. So talk with Jesus (through prayer) and walk with Him (by obeying His rules) today and forever.

A KID'S TIP

If you walk with Jesus every day, you'll never lose your way.

Begin to know Him now, and finish never.
Oswald Chambers

A believer comes to Christ; a disciple follows after Him.
Vance Havner

If I were to ask God how I should live, what would He say?

THE QUICK ANSWER:

Be fair, be a good neighbor, be kind, and loyal.

How to Live

But he's already made it plain how to live, what to do, what God is looking for in men and women. It's quite simple: Do what is fair and just to your neighbor, be compassionate and loyal in your love, and don't take yourself too seriously—take God seriously.

Micah 6:8 MSG

Life is a gift from God. Your job is to unwrap that gift, to use it wisely, and to give thanks to the Giver.

Are you going to treat this day (and every one hereafter) as a special gift to be enjoyed and celebrated? You should—and if you really want to please God, that's exactly what you will do.

A KID'S TIP

Life is a wonderful gift from God. Don't forget to thank the Giver.

God's riches are beyond anything we could ask or even dare to imagine! If my life gets gooey and stale, I have no excuse.

Barbara Johnson

Life is a glorious opportunity.

Billy Graham

I know God has given me special gifts. How should I use them?

THE QUICK ANSWER:
Keep searching for the things you like to do and the things you're good at. Then, keep improving your skills and dedicate your work to God.

Gifts from God

God doesn't want us to be shy with his gifts, but bold and loving and sensible.
2 Timothy 1:7 MSG

All people have special gifts—special blessings from God—and you are no exception. Today, make a promise to yourself that you will earnestly seek to discover the talents that God has given you. Then, keep improving those talents and make them grow. Finally, share your gifts with the world. After all, the best way to say "Thank You" for God's gifts is to use them.

A KID'S TIP

God has given you a special set of amazing gifts. Your job is to use those gifts now, and to use them for God's glory.

The Lord has abundantly blessed me all of my life. I'm not trying to pay Him back for all of His wonderful gifts; I just realize that He gave them to me to give away.

Lisa Whelchel

When God crowns our merits, he is crowning nothing other than his gifts.

St. Augustine

What does the Bible say about the example that I should set for other kids?

THE QUICK ANSWER:
Since you're a Christian, you should act like one. And when you do, your friends will notice.

Be a Good Example

In everything set them an example by doing what is good.
Titus 2:7 NIV

What kind of example are you? Are you the kind of person who shows other people what it means to be kind and forgiving? Hopefully so!!!

How hard is it to say a kind word? Not very! How hard is it to accept someone's apology? Usually not too hard. So today, be a good example for others to follow. Because God needs people, like you, who are willing to stand up and be counted for Him. And that's exactly the kind of example you should try to be.

A KID'S TIP

Your friends are watching: so be the kind of example that God wants you to be—be a good example.

A man ought to live so that everybody knows he is a Christian, and most of all, his family ought to know.

D. L. Moody

Our walk counts far more than our talk, always!

George Mueller

God wants us to show our faith to others. How can I do this?

THE QUICK ANSWER:
By being kind and gracious to others.

Courtesy Matters

Dear friend, when you extend hospitality to Christian brothers and sisters, even when they are strangers, you make the faith visible.

3 John 1:5 MSG

Did Christ instruct us in matters of etiquette and courtesy? Of course He did. Christ's instructions are clear: "In everything, therefore, treat people the same way you want them to treat you, for this is the Law and the Prophets" (Matthew 7:12 NASB). Jesus did not say, "In some things, treat people as you wish to be treated." And, He did not say, "From time to time, treat others with kindness." Christ said that we should treat others as we wish to be treated in every aspect of our daily lives. This, of course, is a tall order indeed, but as Christians, we are commanded to do our best.

A KID'S TIP

The next time you're standing in line, don't try to push ahead of your neighbors. After all, if you don't want other people breaking in line in front of you, then you shouldn't break in line in front of them!

Courtesy is contagious.
Marie T. Freeman

Only the courteous can love, but it is love that makes them courteous.
C. S. Lewis

Everybody needs heroes. Who should be my most important hero?

THE QUICK ANSWER:
Jesus.

Following Christ's Example

For I have given you an example that you also should do just as I have done for you.
John 13:15 HCSB

Who was the greatest example and the most amazing teacher in the history of the world? Jesus was .. and He still is! Jesus teaches us how to live, how to behave, and how to worship. Now, it's up to each of us, as Christians, to learn the important lessons that Jesus can teach.

Someday soon, you will have learned everything that Jesus has to teach you, right? WRONG!!!! Jesus will keep teaching you important lessons throughout your life. And that's good, because all of us, kids and grown-ups alike, have lots to learn . . . especially from the Master . . . and the Master, of course, is Jesus.

A KID'S TIP

Start learning about Jesus, and keep learning about Him as long as you live. His story never grows old, and His teachings never fail.

Sold for thirty pieces of silver, he redeemed the world.
R. G. Lee

When you can't see him, trust him. Jesus is closer than you ever dreamed.
Max Lucado

What does the Bible say about money?

THE QUICK ANSWER:

The Bible says that if you love money, you're making a big mistake.

Don't Worship Money!

For the love of money is a root of all kinds of evil, and by craving it, some have wandered away from the faith and pierced themselves with many pains.

1 Timothy 6:10 HCSB

One of the easiest idols to worship is the idol we call money. Some people will do almost anything to get more money—don't you dare be one of them!

The Bible teaches this important lesson: it's not good to be too concerned about money or the stuff that money can buy. So don't worry too much about the things you can buy in stores. Worry more about obeying your parents and obeying your Heavenly Father—that's what's really important.

A KID'S TIP

Would you like to be a little happier? The Bible says that if you become a more generous person, you'll become a happier person, too. So don't spend all your money . . . Give some of it away!

Christians have become victims of one of the most devious plots Satan ever created—the concept that money belongs to us and not to God.

Larry Burkett

If a person gets his attitude toward money straight, it will help straighten out almost every other area of his life.

Billy Graham

How can I know what's right?

THE QUICK ANSWER:

Listen to your conscience. It will tell you right from wrong.

Your Conscience Will Tell You What to Do

They show that in their hearts they know what is right and wrong.

Romans 2:15 ICB

God gave you something called a conscience: some people describe it as a little voice, but really, it's a feeling—it's a feeling that tells you whether something is right or wrong. Your conscience will usually tell you what to do and when to do it. Pay attention to that feeling, and trust it.

If you slow down and listen to your conscience, you'll usually stay out of trouble. And if you listen to your conscience, it won't be so hard to control your own behavior. Why? Because most of the time, your conscience already knows right from wrong. So don't be in such a hurry to do things. Instead of "jumping right in," listen to your conscience. In the end, you'll be very glad you did.

A KID'S TIP

If you're not sure it's the right thing to do . . . listen to your conscience and talk to your parents.

To go against one's conscience is neither safe nor right. Here I stand. I cannot do otherwise.
Martin Luther

Guilt is a healthy regret for telling God one thing and doing another.
Max Lucado

Where is the best place to find what I should do and be when I grow up?

THE QUICK ANSWER:
Ask Jesus.

Knowing Jesus

Jesus Christ is the same yesterday, today, and forever.

Hebrews 13:8 NCV

There's really no way around it: If you want to know God, you need to know His Son. And that's good, because getting to know Jesus can—and should—be a wonderful experience.

Jesus has offered to share the gifts of everlasting life and everlasting love with the world . . . and with you. If you make mistakes, He'll still be your friend. If you behave badly, He'll still love you. If you feel sad, He can help you feel better.

Jesus has an amazing love for you, so welcome Him into your heart today. When you do, you'll always be grateful that you did.

A KID'S TIP

The Truth with a capital "T":
Jesus is the Truth,
and that's the truth!

No Jesus, no peace;
Know Jesus, know peace!

Anonymous

When we are in a situation where Jesus is all we have, we soon discover He is all we really need.

Gigi Graham Tchividjian

Serve him completely and willingly,
because the Lord knows
what is in everyone's mind.
He understands everything you think.
If you go to him for help,
you will get an answer.

—

1 Chronicles 28:9 NCV

To have courage for whatever comes in life
—everything lies in that.
ST. TERESA OF AVILA

For Sue, Jon, and Jenny,
the true and pure gifts of my life

All Scripture citations throughout this book are from *St. Joseph Edition of the New American Bible* (New York: Catholic Book Publishing Company, 1992).

Some passages written by the author and included in this book first appeared in much shorter and different versions in the periodicals *Living Faith*, published by Creative Communications for the Parish, and the *St. Louis Review*, the newspaper of the Archdiocese of St. Louis, Missouri.

Second printing 2010

TWENTY-THIRD PUBLICATIONS
A Division of Bayard
One Montauk Avenue, Suite 200
New London, CT 06320
(860) 437-3012 or (800) 321-0411
www.23rdpublications.com

ISBN 978-1-58595-785-9
Library of Congress Catalog Card Number: 2010920814
Printed in the U.S.A.

Contents

Acknowledgments

Thanks, first of all, to Sue Givens—my first and best critic and editor. I wouldn't be where I am today as a writer and a man if not for her.

Thanks to my family and friends who have supported me with unending prayers as I face my disease and its challenges. You are too numerous to name and too loving and faithful to fathom.

Thanks to my friend Gloria, who suggested I might have this book in me.

Thanks to my editor at Twenty-Third Publications, Paul Pennick, my sometime lunch companion with the Second Thursday Lunch Club. And hey to Bernadette, Teresa, Tom, and the rest of the gang.

Much gratitude to those songwriters who readily and graciously gave permission to use portions of their lyrics— Carrie Newcomer, Tom Kimmel, Kyle Matthews, and my own collaborator, Phil Cooper.

That One Word

You enter the forest at the darkest point, here there is no path. Where there is a way or a path, it is someone else's path. You are not on your own path. If you follow someone else's way, you are not going to realize your potential.

JOSEPH CAMPBELL

The moment when I got the news from my oncologist is one of those moments etched in time. If you've ever received similar news, which is very probable since you're reading this, you know what I mean. The words tumbled out of her mouth ever so cinematically and slowly. I think I only heard bits and pieces at first...

Blood disease...very rare...we'll need to do some research...run a few more tests...don't know for sure what the...

And then it all hit home with the utterance of one word: chemo-therapy. Everything snapped into focus. I knew what that meant! Or at least I thought I did. A million thoughts flooded my mind in a matter of seconds. How would my life be changed? How would I change? Was I on a fast course toward an early death at forty-seven? Would I get sick, lose my hair, miss time at work? Would I die, or would this be a blip on the radar screen of my life? Was this just "one of those things" that so many people go through and come out the other end whole and better and changed? What would I tell my wife and kids? Those were the questions I asked myself in that brief moment as I sat on the examination table in an ill-fitting gown.

That one moment—and that one word—was the beginning of a new chapter in my life, to be sure, and one that would change me in many ways. For now, almost three years and two long rounds of chemotherapy later, that change has been mostly positive and life-affirming. It hasn't come without its challenges, of course. There have been times of pain, sickness, confusion, and sadness. But it has also been a time of renewal and rebirth spiritually, and that's the reason I decided to write this book.

Admittedly, my journey through this disease and its treatment, which is often worse than the disease itself, has not been as devastating for me as it is, so often, for others. Perhaps that's the biggest blessing of all. For although many have a story to tell, they are not always able to do so because of the toll their disease has taken on them. So, while I can't compare my experience to those who have fought more aggressive diseases such as cancer or leukemia, I do, at least, have an inkling of what they have gone through. And I know that my own journey is not yet over. I've already had several periods of remission followed by a recurrence, and I know this disease will never fully go away.

I think a brotherhood and a sisterhood exist between those who have battled a chronic disease or undergone chemotherapy or other types of treatment. We are kin, of sorts, those of us who have sat in the recliner or lain in the bed while toxic chemicals were injected into our bodies to try and save us or give us more time. We know each other's pain and numbness and exhaustion. We smile at each other when we meet in the hallways or while blood is drawn, because we can relate and because we know.

Many people have asked how I coped with it all. My initial reply may always sound a bit smug, but it's truthful: I coped because I had no choice. One day I thought I was basically healthy, and the next day someone was scheduling my chemotherapy treatments. This is now just part of my life, as it is part of yours. We accept it as we do a new family member.

But how we accept it all is up to us. I have chosen the way of faith and God because I know of no other way that brings peace and gives me a reason to go on. I know that not everyone shares this view of life and eternity, and I respect that. But I cannot imagine any other view for myself, especially as I grapple with issues of life and death.

So I have opted to embrace my disease and its treatment because I really have no other choice. But I have chosen, as a matter of faith and survival, not to embrace it alone, because my arms are not big enough or strong enough for the battle. However, as I hope you will see in the pages that follow, the arms of my God are big enough to encircle both me and the disease that is attacking me. Whatever the outcome, I have decided to live (and someday to die) held in the arms of God. I can't think of a better way.

⁓⟨◊⟩⁓

To some extent my own story doesn't matter, and as I have written above, I can't begin to compare it to the experiences of others (perhaps you) who have fought tougher and more courageous battles. But on the other hand, you have every right to know a little about me if you're going to follow my journey in these pages. You will get to know me and some of my family and friends in the pages that follow, but for now here's a synopsis of the health issues that brought me to this moment in my life.

In the fall of 2006, I began to experience some painful skin rashes and open sores in several areas, as well as a strange collection of bumps on my scalp. I wrote it off for months as a simple dermatological problem that would eventually go away. But after several different dermatologists and numerous kinds of antibiotics, I still hadn't gotten any better. Finally, the last (and smartest, obviously) of the series of dermatologists decided to do a biopsy, and I was given a preliminary diagnosis of Langerhan's cell histiocytosis (LCH), a rare blood disease that affects only about one in 560,000 adults. Sadly, it's a disease that affects children much more often. Still, it's referred to as an "orphan disease," because it affects so few people and thus very little medical research is carried out on it. As I told my friends and family, "I've always liked the idea of being unusual and standing out in a crowd, but this is not what I had in mind!"

Following participation in a dermatological grand rounds (where my rashes were examined by a procession of about fifteen doctors and medical students), the diagnosis was confirmed, and the case was turned over to an oncologist/hematologist. That's when I first heard the word "chemotherapy" and started to get a little scared.

My wife, Sue, was the only person I had told up until this point, but now I faced the reality and the difficulty of telling my two kids and a few close friends, followed by my colleagues at work. Telling Sue and the kids was absolutely the hardest thing I ever had to do, especially when we knew so little about the disease and the prognosis. Sue, a CPA with a brilliant and methodical mind, set to work finding out all she could about the disease and its treatment. I think she was more interested in the details than I was, and it seemed like she knew as much as my doctor did when we met for the first time to discuss treatment.

My daughter Jenny, who was then fifteen (and is now a college freshman studying to become a music teacher), was direct. She asked: "Could you die?" The words cut me to the core—not because she raised the issue of my mortality but because I knew the pain I was causing her at that moment. My son Jon, who was then twenty and away at college, was quieter and more reflective about the whole thing, which is his way. Both of their responses, of course, were valid, authentic, and reflected the differences in their personalities.

The chemotherapy was set to begin as soon as Sue and I returned from a trip to Ireland as chaperons for Jenny's high school choir. On that trip, filled with anxiety about what the future might hold, I received a wonderful, unexpected, and life-giving gift from the girls and the conductor of the choir. I am a composer and lyricist and, unbeknownst to me, a small ensemble of about ten girls had arranged and rehearsed one of my compositions to perform during the concert tour and insisted that I be guest soloist. I wasn't even told about it until the night before the first performance! We performed the song at about a half-dozen different venues, including the majestic St. Patrick's Cathedral in Dublin and the Knock Marian Shrine.

I'm a firm believer in the healing power of music, so the chance to perform with the choir was just what I needed to get my mind off my impending treatment and centered on the peace that I know only God can give. That gift of music was perhaps the first of so many blessings that have come my way from caring, loving friends and—as is sometimes the case—even from complete strangers.

Chemo started the Thursday after we returned—once a week for six weeks at first, and I was only at the treatment center for a couple of hours each time. I also took a steroid called prednisone and some antibiotics. By most comparisons with others fighting cancer or other aggressive diseases, my treatment was fairly mild and didn't produce as many side effects. Still, about ten days after the first treatment I experienced some pretty intense joint pain in my arms, followed by neuropathy in my hands and feet. The pain eventually went away (although it still returns to some extent with each new treatment), but the neuropathy has been a fairly constant companion ever since April 2007. Still, it's more like "something to deal with" than real pain or illness. I could be a lot worse off, I kept telling myself and others.

A week or two later my hair started falling out, especially when I took a shower. I bought a cool, hip hat and waited. My hair quickly got thin and patchy but I never lost it all.

I finished the weekly treatments and transitioned to a six-month maintenance cycle with treatments every three to four weeks. By then the rashes had pretty much gone away and I was feeling pretty good. At the end of the six months, I learned a new word—remission. It meant a break from treatments and a certain, if limited, sense of hope and relief. I also learned that doctors use the word remission instead of "cured" because there's often no way to tell if and when the disease might come back. I took it as a temporary victory and moved on. My hair came back and everybody told me how good I looked.

The only negatives I felt were the unknowns: Will it stay away or will it start creeping back when the treatments stop? Worse yet, will future MRI scans show the presence of the dangerous cells in other places? My skin was a fairly easy organ with which to work, but an occurrence in another, more vital organ could be far more dangerous. The doctor also noted that the disease could leave me more susceptible to tumors and cancers in the future, so I knew in many ways I'd be dealing with this for the rest of my life.

Indeed, about six months later, a few of the rashes began to reappear, and I thought for sure I was headed to treatment again. I went on a men's retreat at my parish and geared up for the next onslaught. I talked about it. I prayed about it. I wrote about it. I went to confession and bawled my eyes out about my sins and weaknesses. But almost as quickly as the rashes started, they went away. Sometimes your body can take care of itself, my oncologist said. Others pointed to the power of prayer. I was thankful for both points of view.

However, less than a year later the rashes were back again and there was no doubt I needed to go back to "Chemoworld," as I had begun to call it. So, as I write this introduction, I have just completed another initial round of treatment and am headed back into maintenance therapy. Currently, it looks like I'll be doing this for a long time. I feel like an old car, getting serviced and ready for another 50,000 miles. But I'm still running, and life is good.

That's my story, or at least part of it. What follows—the stories, the reflections, the prayers, are a more important part of what I want to share with you. I hope you find something in here that helps you, something you can relate to, something that brings you to your knees or makes you laugh or cry or throw up your arms in worship and adoration of the One who made us all. I pray you can come to embrace what is happening, even as it makes you sick and rocks your world. From the depths of Chemoworld, I hope I can help you in some small way to find and see God. He knows you're there. He knows what you're going through. He knows you by name.

This is my faith. This is what I have learned to embrace. And that's where I'll start.

A few last thoughts as you begin:

I have used the masculine "he" throughout the book when referring to God, not because I really believe God is masculine (or feminine) but because that's my own personal tradition and preference. I hope it's not a stumbling stone for you—I certainly don't mean it to be. Some contemporary conventions for dealing with this issue, such as alternating between the masculine and feminine or just using the word God over and over, even when it becomes cumbersome to the reader (and the writer!) seem to be even larger stumbling blocks. So I've settled on this.

At the end of each chapter I've included three recurring kinds of questions (or "prompts") that you can use for quiet reflection, journaling, or good conversation among friends. I hope you find them useful as a starting place for your own personal journey into your disease, treatment, and survival.

Also at the end of each chapter you'll find a short prayer. I'm a believer in short prayers. My favorite is: "Lord, help me. Amen." Again, I offer these prayers as a starting point. Use them however you want. Whether you read each prayer as a punctuation mark to the chapter before you turn out the light, or you use it as the beginning of a time of personal prayer and contemplation, I hope it helps.

1

Embracing the Mystery

*True faith has nothing to do with jollying people along. It has
everything to do with facing the fact that things may be an utter
and total mess, may be on the verge of going to hell in a hand-
basket, with the conviction that God is at work in the mess.*

MICHAEL HIMES

For some mysterious reason, my body has decided to throw a
wrench into my otherwise very good life. Even though I've been basically healthy for a while now, and my treatments haven't overly dis-
rupted my everyday life, this disease and its treatment have changed
me in many ways—some of which I may never even realize. And even
though my doctors and nurses are wonderful, and I'm surrounded
by caring friends and family and all their prayers, there is no doubt
that this whole thing encircles and encompasses me. It is, to a great
extent, what I have become. It is who I am. Or at least that's how I
feel on many days. No one can really say why I have this disease. It is
the great and brooding mystery of my life. So I've been thinking a lot
lately about mystery.

Shortly after my first chemo treatments began, I remember going to church one Sunday feeling like one of those proverbial horses that have been "rode hard and put up wet." It was not one of my better days. I ached all over. I was listless. I didn't want to move or think or do anything. I certainly wasn't in the mood to put much effort into praying and singing. I really just didn't want to be there. I would have preferred to have stayed in bed.

But since I was already there, I decided to challenge God, who had given me this mysterious disease. (OK, I knew at some deep level that God doesn't give people diseases, but that was beside the point at that moment.) So I prayed something like, "OK, God, hit me with your best shot. Give me one good reason why I should be here today instead of at home curled up in my nice warm bed with the covers pulled over my head."

I knew it was a silly thing to do, but that was just the way I felt that day, and somewhere inside me I knew God would understand. I didn't really think he would respond but, of course, he proceeded to do just that. From the opening song to the Scripture readings to the homily to the communion hymn, I was cut to the quick with the wisdom and the love and the grace of God that day. Every lyric, every prayer, every nugget of Scripture seemed to be spoken and sung for me alone. If not for the power of community around me, I could have been having a conversation with God all by myself. My God, I thought, you are indeed mysterious and, as we all know, you work in mysterious ways.

So I became intrigued by and drawn to the idea that God, all in all, is a mystery. It's a good mystery, of course. God's a huge, divine, holy, sacred mystery, and the power of that mystery fills my life. But God's still a mystery, and I've decided to embrace that. My daily prayer has become, "Surprise me today, Lord. Reveal to me some of the mystery and meaning behind all that's happening to me."

Since then, I've found myself inundated and inebriated with mystery, as well as by a string of confusing emotions like fear, worry, and a few moments of anger. I have had long and good talks with friends and family. And here's what I've figured out so far: This mysterious disease with its equally mysterious treatment will run its course, one way or another. My doctors and nurses are very positive about the prospects of controlling it. So am I. That's my story and I'm stickin' to it.

But I know there's a flip side to that coin, too. None of us, whether we are carrying around a life-threatening disease or not, know the balance of our life. We don't know if we have a day left or decades. And I believe life is just too precious to spend very much time contemplating the end of it. So in the meantime, I've decided to embrace the mystery of the whole thing instead of running scared. I've been pretty good at telling others to "keep the faith" over the years when such things happen to them, so now it's time to follow my own advice.

I'm embracing the wonder of modern medicine and the wisdom of my doctors, along with the frightening notions behind words no one likes to hear or say, like "chemotherapy" and "cancer treatment center." I'm embracing the power of a healing and life-giving evening of good food, music, conversation, and lots of laughter with my very best friends. Especially laughter. I simply refuse to stop laughing, especially at myself.

More than all this and above all else, I'm embracing the mystery of God's presence in my life, delighting and in awe of the fact that he knows me and has called me by name. As my friend Fr. Gary once said to me, "Never forget that Jesus is crazy about you, Steve." That was powerful for me to hear, even though I already thought I knew it. It helped me remember that God is not just "out there," hovering and lingering over us like a zookeeper. God is crazy about us. As much as I am crazy about my wife and kids, God is way crazier about us all. You've got to like that.

My God is a God of mystery, but not because he is removed and distant and uncaring. In the words of author and priest Michael Himes, "God is mystery not because God is so distant but because God is so terribly close."

My God is the God of all I see and touch and feel. He is the God of all that is coursing through my veins—the good and the bad, the disease and the medicine. God counts not only my days but also the ever-diminishing hairs on my head, my footsteps, and my breaths. He is the God of rare blood diseases and cancer centers and chemotherapy. This is my faith, and my faith is in the mystery of God.

Name five things... about God that make him mysterious to you.

Ask yourself... do these mysteries bother me, or can I bring myself to embrace them as part of my understanding of God? How can I do that?

When was the last time... you felt like Jesus was crazy about you?

God, you are a great and mysterious force in my life. Teach me to understand and embrace your mysteries as I walk the path that unfolds before me. Help me to sense you beside me, my constant companion on the journey, rather than spending time worrying about what might or might not happen around the next bend. Engage me in the present, secure in your presence. Amen.

2

In Chemoworld…

*Prayer and love are learned in the hour when prayer has
become impossible and your heart has turned to stone.*

THOMAS MERTON

The moment the elevator door opens on the seventh floor
and I enter the treatment center, I feel as if I am in a different world
from the one where I spend the rest of my days and nights. It's different for a number of reasons: the place itself, my fellow travelers in
treatment, and my own state of mind and spirit. Chemoworld, I like
to call it.

The center, although part of a massive, modern, and sprawling
medical center in St. Louis' urban and trendy central west end, is generally quiet, and the people around me seem (again, generally) pretty
unaffected, at least for a time, by the world outside the walls of the
center. The economy may be falling apart, political candidates and
parties may be railing against each other, and war may be raging in
far-flung regions of the world, but for a few hours none of that matters as much as the battle being fought between life and death in our

13

own bodies. As killer chemicals are sent racing and screaming into our bodies like tiny Kamikaze pilots on a mission, we're in a different world.

I realize that, so far at least, I have been luckier than many in that my treatments are relatively quick affairs. I'm usually in and out within an hour or two and, while the treatments themselves make me weak and achy for a few days, I'm well aware that many others are not as fortunate. All that could change for me tomorrow, of course. For now, though, I am blessed.

But whatever the length and intensity of my time in Chemoworld, it's safe to say I wouldn't wish the experience on anyone. Still, I have tried to make the best of the time as a short period of quiet, introspection, meditation, and prayer. I realize that many of my fellow travelers to Chemoworld find comfort and peace by having a loved one at their side during treatment. That time of intimacy between two people can be extremely valuable and needed. My wife asked me if I wanted her to accompany me, but I have opted to go it alone, partially so that I wouldn't be burdening her with one more obligation (although obviously she doesn't see it that way), but additionally because I enjoy and need the quiet time to think, pray, or read. That's my choice and I realize it's not everyone's, and I also know that my own desire to have her there beside me might change over time and circumstances.

Chemoworld is no day at the beach, and neither is it a monastery or retreat center. For many it is worse than the disease itself. But I have found that it can be a brief respite and time apart. So if I'm not the chattiest of patients with my caregivers and the other patients around me, it's because I have come to appreciate and savor the relative quiet. There's nothing I enjoy better than good conversation, but I'm also not one for small talk. I don't talk much to my barber or the person next to me on an airplane, either. That's just me.

In any case, this whole experience in Chemoworld has been a good reminder of something that I know well but often forget: God calls us—and even encourages us through the example of Jesus—to make time to get away and spend time alone with him. These "desert" experiences are essential for our spiritual growth, and I have found that to be particularly true during the time of illness and treatment. In fact, "desert" or "wilderness" may just be the perfect metaphors for the experience of chemotherapy.

We go into the desert to be cleansed and refreshed. We go into the desert to relocate our center and re-establish our bonds with our inner life and our God who resides there. Many years ago while on a retreat, I learned from a Marianist priest and writer, Quentin Hakenewerth, the importance of slowing and quieting down so we can find our centers. In a graphic of concentric circles, he showed us all the things in our lives that scream at us and demand attention. At the center was our spiritual self, our soul, waiting quietly and patiently for everything else to quiet down so it could speak. We can only hear that most inner part of ourselves when we move away from the world, when we quiet the screaming voices of advertisers and co-workers and even family members, and go off by ourselves to listen to that quiet inner voice. For it is there we hear our true selves, it is there we hear and can understand what God is saying and what it is he might be calling us to do. Listen closely. Can you hear him?

*Name five things…*that scream for your attention and distract you from hearing the voice of God and your own soul.

*Ask yourself…*when and where can I find the time to get away, quiet myself, and learn to listen for these true voices in my life? Could I do it during chemotherapy?

*When was the last time…*you had a clear sense of listening to your soul or the voice of God? What did you hear?

*G*od, take me by the hand as I walk through the wilderness that is this disease and its treatment. Never leave me alone. Lead me to a quiet place and then help me silence both the world around me and the battle for my attention that rages inside my own head. Quiet me, focus me, and allow me to hear the still, small voice that I know to be you speaking to my soul. Help me to see that this is my truest self, and help me to respond to the call that I hear in these special moments. Give me the guidance I need to face this disease with courage and hope. Speak to me today, my Lord and my God, my center and my all. Amen.

3

Grappling with Life's Numb Moments

*There are only two ways to live your life. One is
as though nothing is a miracle. The other is as
though everything is a miracle.*

ALBERT EINSTEIN

⁂

Over the course of my treatment, my chemotherapy drugs have caused what is known as "peripheral neuropathy." In short, my hands and feet are numb. My size-ten feet tingle when I walk, which sounds a little like a line from a Broadway musical, but it's far less entertaining. When the neuropathy first kicked in, I kept dropping things (most memorably a full glass of milk all over the kitchen floor) because my sense of touch had changed with the deadening of the nerves in my hands. I learned to laugh while I cleaned up the messes, and my wife learned to never just hand me a drink without asking, "You got it?"

All in all, I guess it's a pretty small price to pay for the unrelenting work these killer-chemicals are doing to beat the disease into remission, so I'm not really complaining. But nevertheless this numbness is a strange and constant reminder of the whole kit and caboodle— disease and treatment rolled into one unique experience.

Mostly I ignore the neuropathy since there's no point in battling it. But there have been moments when I have been tempted to give in to this numbness in my extremities and let it take over the rest of my life. Sometimes it feels like it would be easier to just give up and give in, even when I know that it's not true. Such was the case one day not long ago when I was at church. There I sat, feeling like I'd really rather be home, watching the Cardinals game, putting my tingling feet up on the ottoman and allowing my peripheral neuropathy to ooze in from the edges and take over the rest of my body and soul. I was numb all over—inside and out—and wasn't in the mood to feel much of anything. At that moment I was almost ready to surrender, to throw in the towel and become a victim to the disease. And "victim" was a word I had sworn to myself I would never use when describing myself and my battle with this disease.

So it's a good thing that my faith, however fragile it can be from time to time, doesn't rely on how I feel. For my faith, I believe, takes me further and deeper and closer to the truth than any feelings I might have on any given day.

So instead of walking out of the church, I settled into my pew to see what God might have to say to me on that fine autumn day. The reading (from Wisdom, chapter 9) grabbed me like an old mother cat grabs a newborn kitten—seemingly roughly but actually gently by the scruff of the neck. I sat up straighter and paid closer attention.

"Who can know God's counsel," it began, "or who can conceive what the Lord intends?" I swallowed hard. Who knows, indeed? The lector continued: "For the corruptible body burdens the soul..."

Even as the words about my corruptible body were spoken (for surely, I thought, these words were meant for me alone), I felt the